AF317018

FROM FEAR
TO FEARLESS

YOU CAN HAVE IT ALL

TEARA TAYLOR

Dedication

It's time to get out of your head. All the limits you think you are bound by only exist in your mind. In the real world, it is really easy to achieve whatever you want and get to whichever destination you desire.

You can do it all; you only have to start. To start, you need the feeling that you can do it. If you find it risky, know that fear is worth the risk. You can set boundaries if it feels as though you are giving too much of yourself. Don't give up when it gets hard because that's the moment when you can see the results and experience growth.

I believe you can have it all—a satisfying relationship, job, family, finances, or whatever you want. *Just not all at once.* See, working on yourself takes time. Acknowledge what makes you afraid but go after it fearlessly.

You got this! I believe in you.

I dedicate this book to every one of my readers, including you, who are facing fear. I dedicate this book to your growth.

This book will help you transform yourself from Fear to Fearless.

Your biggest cheerleader,

Teara

TABLE OF CONTENTS

1

Fear of Commitment

Fear of commitment is the fear of long-lasting relationships. This fear can lead to difficulty forming or maintaining friendships or romantic attachments. In fact, it is what keeps most people from pursuing romantic ties.

Many people suffering from this fear don't even realize how intense it can be. It is a psychologically recognized fear, termed *gamophobia* from the Greek *gamos*, meaning marriage, and *phobia*, meaning fear.

Fear of Commitment in Relationships

Fear of commitment in relationships comes from hurt and pain. If you've been hurt in the past, it takes courage to move forward when you are afraid. Even when you tell yourself that whatever happens happens for the best, deep down you are likely to be hurting. You may try to ignore the pain, but that doesn't stop it from existing.

As a young adult, I gave dating a shot like anyone else. Though I wanted a new relationship, I would fail to commit. I would always be half in/half out. Somehow, I developed a subconscious idea that all my relationships would fail. Maybe I thought that, because most of the relationships around me did fail, mine would have to as well. My female friends described to me the various ways in which they had been dumped. My male friends shared stories of why their romantic relationships didn't last. I heard many more stories and saw several relationships end right in front of my eyes.

All this negativity left me confused in the beginning. I couldn't understand how two people who seemed to be wildly in love would go on to speak so harshly about each other. One month they would want to spend every minute with this person; the next month they would be avoiding places where they might run into that person who was now their ex. How does one go from planning a wedding with someone to moving to a different city just to avoid them?

My confusion soon turned to fear. I didn't want to be in a position where I would loathe a person I claimed to love or have the same thing happen to them. I didn't want to uproot my life just because the chance of running into someone was too painful to bear.

I personally didn't have to experience a breakup, but it hurt me to see others hurt. The possibility that someone so close to me would become a stranger didn't sit well with me. I didn't like it when my friends would cry or shut themselves in the house as they tried to get over their ex. It took them months, and sometimes over a year, to even look at another potential love interest. I didn't feel their pain as they felt it, but it was hard seeing them suffer. I mourned their loss. I didn't want to go through it myself. I didn't think I could tolerate it as my friends did.

Past experience is the number one cause of developing a fear of commitment. It complicates things because we are not afraid of commitment itself; we are only afraid of getting hurt again.

In a way, fear of commitment helps us heal. It keeps us from committing to something we are not yet ready for. Relationships are about growth; love makes us evolve. In fact, we change whether or not we are in a relationship. But not everyone's growth looks the same. A person's growth is a deeply personal experience that onlookers rarely understand. It is never a linear process, and it drains a lot of mental and emotional energy. It can be painful, too, but without visible scars or wounds, which makes it confusing for the one experiencing it and the people around them.

Allowing someone, such as your partner, to see you being your most vulnerable self as you experience growth is scary. You never know how they will react. You might not know if they experienced any personal growth themselves. If so, how did they handle it? Will they understand your growth and how you achieve it? Or will they find your growth phase insufferable?

You can only receive answers to these questions after you go through a growth phase in a relationship with someone. There is no other way. So, getting into a relationship is risky. It requires us to endanger our vulnerability, jeopardize our privacy, and put us on the line for developing a fear of commitment.

But here's the thing: we cannot find love if we keep pushing others away and never take a chance. To find happiness, we have no choice but to overcome our fear.

As mentioned earlier, I have experienced the fear of commitment. I was scared of being vulnerable and expressing my feelings. I couldn't open up in front of anyone romantically. Vulnerability takes courage, and all my courage had gone into hiding deep inside me for fear of getting hurt again.

I could see the signs of fear of commitment taking over me. I'm a very friendly person, so it is easy for me to make friends. But even if I was on a date and liked the person, I wouldn't let it develop beyond friendship. I would even tell them this outright. I would say, "We can only be friends. We can talk on the phone and continue to go out, but only as friends."

Initially, my dates would think I wanted to take it slow, and they would agree. Eventually, the guy would ask, "Why can't we go further than being friends?" To this, I would always reply, "I enjoy our friendship more. I would rather have you as a friend than a date. If it doesn't work out, we will have nothing."

I would confess my feelings to myself but never aloud. It was easy to express myself in my journal, but I never wanted to express myself to another person. I was trying to enjoy their company but only while eliminating the fear of getting hurt.

I wanted to start over with those I liked. I wanted to reintroduce myself. But I was always second-guessing my own worth for not being good enough.

Eventually, I grew used to being alone. I believed that I was committed to myself, and that meant being committed to avoiding the hurt of a lost love. I stayed this way for so long that I became used to being alone. Starting from the fear of commitment, I had reached a point where I also feared sharing my life with someone.

I believe it is a privilege to share one's life with someone, and even more so to be chosen by someone to share their life. Yet back then I didn't want to grant this privilege to someone who might later disappear from my life. Moreover, I wasn't ready to accept such a great privilege from someone else.

In my life with my friends and family, I have observed that love only grows. The more you know someone, the more you grow to love them for their unique traits and personality. Of course, in this generality, I do not include people who hide their truth so they can manipulate and hurt others. But I knew that my friends were kind and good people. And even though some of my friends had unfortunate experiences in the dating world, I also found most of their significant others to be good people.

I have seen my friends think of their exes fondly years after breaking up. While this only happened after enough time had passed and they had moved on or even found new partners, I couldn't help wondering how it must have felt when the breakup was still fresh. I couldn't imagine myself going through such a thing. *I couldn't commit to something that had the potential of bringing me such pain!* The way out was simple: don't commit to anyone. Ever. I only realized I was suffering from fear of commitment when I wouldn't commit to anyone but myself despite a strong desire to be with someone. I didn't believe that a stranger could love me for who I was the way my parents loved each other. I knew the comparison wasn't justified, but I set my bar for love high according to the way they loved me.

And this whole time, I knew I was hesitant and admitted my fear. I never denied any of it. I would stand in front of the mirror looking at myself and thinking, *I cannot wait to be in a loving and supportive relationship.* I knew I was going to be good at it. I had so much to offer. I had so many ideas for holiday gifts, date nights, meeting parents, and vacations. I knew how to have difficult conversations. I would even practice them, watching my tone and body language. I would smile at the thought of being in a loving relationship. Yet, in that same breath, I would remind myself, *just focus on yourself.*

I used this time to reflect on myself. Whether I was in a relationship or not, I was happy and enjoyed my life. A long-term relationship was on my list, but I wanted to change my mind set before finding one. I had to do it, since I knew I couldn't commit to someone until I overcame my fears. I wanted to be strong enough to enjoy both the good and bad parts of a romantic relationship. True love is when you can cherish the people you invite into your life, even if they cannot stay forever. This is how we enjoy the best relationships of our lives. Besides the blood bonds, we even look back on friendships that fall apart fondly. We miss our friends, even when they are no longer our friends, and cherish the memories we made with them.

Romantic love shouldn't be different—that's what I have always believed. I wanted to reach the mental stage where I didn't face any issue applying my beliefs and values to love.

I stopped watching television and replaced it with educational books about relationships. In my observation, T.V. does not portray relationships realistically. The same with romantic novels. They both portray an exaggerated idea of love that is rare in the real world.

Still, I did believe that love and romance exist. I had grown up seeing a loving relationship between my parents. People did love each other like crazy, but those romantic gestures and moments formed less than one percent of any relationship. Real life and real relationships existed in the other ninety-nine percent, where both people retained their personal lives, professional careers, life goals, hobbies, parents, siblings, and friends. It existed in caring for each other's preferences when cooking food at home and understanding each other's routines when planning a night out. If the couple lived together, a real relationship existed in dealing with finances, dividing house chores, and giving each other space.

Grasping a true understanding of what love and relationships really mean allowed me to see them for what they really are: just one part of life. Not the center of life or the whole life, as T.V. and romance novels portray them to be. It allowed me to understand that only when I could be happy in other aspects of my life could I be happy in my romantic life. I realized that being by yourself is not a bad thing. I wanted to be in a relationship one day, but I wasn't going to overthink it. I decided to enjoy life in my own way at its own pace. I truly believe this change in approach from preparing myself to be happy in a relationship to focusing on being happy in my individual life cured me of my fear of commitment. It allowed me to let love happen at its own pace. I wasn't going to do anything about it.

This doesn't mean that I wouldn't approach someone I found attractive at a party, or that I wouldn't go on dates set up for me by my friends. It just means that I will allow things to happen naturally, without pushing or stopping them in any way.

How to Identify the Fear of Commitment

I'm always amazed at how life works. We each have a list of what we want and need in a relationship. But do we comply with these lists ourselves?

Values, integrity, financial stability, good communication skills, confidence—our list of desirable attributes can go on and on. I'm sure if we saw the lists made by others searching for a partner, we would discover that we need several improvements, too. That's totally fine. It's good to list, plan, and pray. However, it's also good to be flexible. Plans and lists can change over time with priorities; prayers can also take a little longer to be answered.

I remember how my fear of commitment made me put together a list that was imperative for a guy to check off if I were to even see him. It included: family man, supportive, loving, honest, caring, independent, good communication skills, trust, humor, accountability, helpful, protective, well-mannered, and many other traits. I didn't want to have to train anyone, either. Of course, every individual has unique needs and partners can coach each other to make the relationship better, but nobody can change another person. I was also scared of not being able to check off the boxes a guy would have on his list. I wanted to play fair, fear or no fear.

However, my confidence in myself would make me say, *It's not you; it's me.* I would tell myself that it didn't even hurt me to be alone. I would go on dates and know halfway through that it wasn't going to go anywhere, so I wouldn't let it go past dinner.

To me, the fear of commitment wasn't difficult to identify but exhausting to carry. It was like carrying an unnecessary burden. I would sometimes ask myself, *How long are you going to carry it? There's nothing holding you back but the past, which you have already learned from and made peace with. It is time to open up and create new experiences.* I was already an open and loud person, though. I have always loved socializing. I'm very outgoing, friendly, and talkative, but when it came to romantic partnerships, I would suddenly become quiet and private when talking to other people. I wanted to be good at relationships like I was good at everything else; in fact, even more so. I have always considered romantic relationships to be special, and I was so scared to fail.

As an overthinker, I have always been too cautious and calculated. I trained myself for the unknown so I would never lash out or say something wrong. I knew how to handle any situation, including being lied to or cheated on by my significant other. I never wanted to yell or raise my voice if such a thing came to fruition. I wanted to have a conversation with grace, listening actively and responding thoughtfully. This may sound like a good plan, and it really is good to think about healthy ways to handle possible relationship problems. The trouble was that my fear of commitment made me assume I would be cheated on when I hadn't ever had a second date! Though it helped me prepare and maintain my standards, I knew it was—even if only a little—irrational. So I tried to let it out.

I didn't just want a boyfriend; I wanted a commitment. So I wasn't going to rush it. I wanted to keep my romantic life private until I was ready to commit to a person for the rest of my life, and he to me. I started reading books and listening to podcasts and sermons on relationships and romantic love. I had already known that I was going to be good at it, but I wanted to learn about the things I didn't know how to do, like opening up. I even practiced deep breathing techniques so I could control my feelings if I felt overwhelmed. It wasn't going to be easy, and I knew it. Finally, one day I wrote in my journal, *I'm scared to be in a relationship, but the fear stops now.*

How to Get Over the Fear and Become Ready to Commit

Let me say it again: being honest with yourself is not easy. It doesn't happen overnight. It can take days, weeks, months, or even years. It took me about three and a half years to overcome my fear of commitment. During this time, I had many moments of doubt and hesitation. I would tell people I was working on myself, which was true. But I was also buying more time before I put myself out there.

It can be difficult to talk about your fears, too. I wouldn't talk about my fear of commitment even with people closest to me. I would try to divert the conversation whenever my mom asked me when I was going to get into a relationship. I didn't want her to know I had a fear of commitment, but my mom knew it well. She always knew the answers before she even asked the questions.

With my friends, I always said I wanted to be in a relationship but didn't feel ready. They would tell me to take my time and not rush into it. They were very positive about it. We would talk for hours, discussing what we did or didn't want in a relationship. Those conversations made me feel hopeful, even when I felt lonely.

It was true that I wasn't in a rush. But it was also true that I was using time as an excuse to allow my fear of commitment to persist.

If you fear commitment, don't rush to get over it and find a partner. Continue to build and grow yourself so you'll be ready when the right person comes into your life. When you are ready to learn, love, grow, and evolve, you can then become the right person for the right person. Remember, love and relationships are essential parts of life, but they are not your entire life. You cannot expect to sort out your life only after you have someone. Your life is your responsibility; your happiness is your responsibility. Nobody fixes your life, nor is it anyone's responsibility.

I have come to realize that relationships fail and lead to fear of commitment when the things we expect from them are impossible. Two people stay in a relationship when their values, goals, and ideologies are similar. Nobody can change the vital parts of who they are, the characteristics that define them, just to meet someone else's expectations. These things cannot be compromised. So, for two people to be together for the long term, they must each be a whole person on their own. When they join together, their happiness and passion for life will then double. But they can only do this if they are whole to begin with.

We each have to find happiness and contentment with our life on a general level, too. When we are unhappy with our life, nothing about it will excite us, not even a loving relationship. Similarly, we can find joy in the mundane when we are content with our lives. Our partners don't have to get us flowers every day to make us happy. When we are happy, we can look at flowers in a park and smile.

The idea of a person coming into our life and fixing everything comes from princess stories where a damsel in distress meets a prince charming or knight in shining armor. But reality is much different than the fictional stories we tell children to keep their view of the world optimistic. That doesn't mean we can't enjoy or find inspiration in these stories as adults, nor does it mean that we become pessimistic, hopeless individuals. But we have to develop a realistic point of view once we grow up. We must realize that we are our own heroes, and nobody else can fix our lives. Our life partners are only meant to assist us in our journey of personal growth, and we can only do the same for them.

It's okay not to be an expert at relationships. But you must be willing to listen. It's okay to start over. Just be careful that you don't commit to something that doesn't serve you in the long term.

You must actively listen to understand. Stop spending time questioning everything. I started focusing on myself and making sure I was fully charged at 100% before I plugged myself into someone else. I say this from my own growth experience and getting over my fears. As I grew, I started to understand that I may be uncomfortable being in a healthy, positive relationship. It wasn't that every date or relationship I had was negative. It was me who went in with a negative approach every time, sabotaging any chances the relationship had just to protect myself from fear of the unknown. Of course, it kept me from finding good things as much as it kept me from getting hurt. Eventually, I learned that I could not control everything and that I could be missing out on an amazing guy because of what I feared.

I've had many negative experiences with men. I've had married guys approach me and men who were in two or more relationships. These experiences instilled fear in me, but I didn't want these experiences to determine what I wanted or hold me back from getting it. I wanted a healthy relationship. Somehow, this basic need is a lot by today's standards. But I decided not to let my fears stop me from having a healthy relationship, and I kept my options open. The result is that I am currently in a relationship that is working for both of us due to honesty, flexibility, and good communication.

A healthy relationship requires give and take. I was listening to Brene Brown, and she described the method of running a relationship by covering for each other. We already were using that in our relationship. But our relationship isn't always 50/50, and that's true for all couples. We stay aware by quantifying where we are at any given time. Thus, if I ask him what percentage he is at and he tells me 30%, I will bring 70% of the kindness, patience, and energy to the relationship. He does the same for me when I am running low. On days when both of our combined energies are not at 100%, and neither of us feels ready to cover for the other, we will recharge and regroup. We spend time apart but text to let the other know that we are there to support in any way possible.

Ultimately, self-care is internal work. I cannot cover patience and kindness for my significant other if I don't offer it to myself first. The same holds true for every other individual in this world. We need to make sure we are enough for ourselves; only then can we offer compassion, love, empathy, patience, and kindness to someone else.

Once you have become ready for a relationship, communication is key. For example, on days when my headspace is full, I communicate to my significant other that I will be going to bed early and won't be available by phone. This is the way to show commitment to someone even when you don't have the energy to be there for them at times. Since our relationship is long distance at the moment, communication has become the number one priority. We know each other's schedules and everything ordinary or extraordinary that happens on a given day. Our biggest win has been both of us taking the lead in communication. Of course, busy schedules and other life events can make us forget about checking in, but we notice it and adjust. It is like having each other's back. It isn't easy, but it's worth the effort.

Communication is essential for every relationship, no matter if the partners are living in the same city or under the same roof. This is because communication honors trust and commitment. It eliminates room for overthinking or second-guessing. It's not always easy, no matter how strong the relationship is, but you must want to put in the effort to enjoy its results.

To experience a healthy and loving relationship and conquer your fear of commitment, here's a simple process to adopt.

- Write out your fears.

- Be honest with yourself about how you feel.

- Talk to someone you trust and who understands your fear.

- I spend time in prayer, journaling, and embracing stillness.

- Enjoy the process of facing your fear and conquering it.

- Visualize your post-fear life and how it would feel.

- Celebrate yourself.

Be aware, however, that there is no telling how long it may take you. The key is to be persistent.

Lesson: Relationships Will Always be Scary

Whenever fear holds me back from something I want to do, I think about the women who don't have a voice, who don't feel seen. They help me realize how fortunate I am to be in a position where the only thing holding me back is my own fear.

Of course, I still have moments when I'm fearful, unsure, scared, or when I overthink, but I do it anyway. I do it not knowing how impactful it will be, how many people will notice, or how successful I will be. I see it as practice until I succeed and become comfortable.

It's still scary, of course. Not all moments of a relationship are happy. There are difficult moments you have to go through to find that happiness again and again. But this work is required in all relationships. Constant happiness would be boring.

Romantic relationships are even scarier because they make you be your most vulnerable self. You can hide your pain and sorrow from friends, siblings, and even parents, but your significant other will know everything about you. They do because they have to account for your preferences in their day-to-day lives. If for any reason they stop doing that, there is nothing you can do.

Being in a relationship is not something that just happens. It's a choice you make every day. Morning and night. Happy and sad. It's not about finding someone who can make you constantly happy. It's about finding someone who is willing to talk through the bad times realistically and openly so you can get back to the good times. The key to finding someone who is willing to grow together with you and contribute to the growth of the relationship is to be open and willing yourself.

Nobody can prove themselves worthy of the hard work a relationship requires unless you give them a chance. But you must also do the same. You must be capable and willing to grow, evolve, love, and commit; to give as much as you receive. All these traits will only show through when you get past fear of commitment.

The Relationship Between Vulnerability and Commitment

Developing the ability to process emotions and acknowledge the pain we're feeling is what vulnerability essentially is. Being vulnerable means we have the power to surrender to our pain, guilt, regret, shame, debilitating feelings, and overwhelming emotions.

Emotional vulnerability requires a lot from us. We're willing to show our real, weaker versions to people we trust and believe in the strength of our relationship to hold it together. Being vulnerable with people has a lot to do with the level of invisible trust we have for them. It's that trust that makes us comfortable opening up and lowering our guard.

It's never easy to be vulnerable with someone, even if you trust them with your life. In all honesty, this is quite justified. The people in our lives love us for who we are, and we have faith that they will continue to do so. However, there is not a single person who doesn't have a side they haven't shown to the public or even their friends. This particular side can restrict us from socializing when it makes us feel like an imposter who doesn't belong. We withhold our reality from the people who love us because we fear they might leave if they find out the truth. The reason we feel this way is that we assign more shame than kindness or understanding to our vulnerability. We believe it's weak, incapable, and not a happy side. We wonder why we should let anyone know how we truly feel when it will only make them think less of us. However, that's just a projection. We believe this of others because we view our own vulnerability this way. Acknowledging emotions is not easy, nor is it convenient. Yet the rewards are worth it.

Nevertheless, we cannot expect to find the answer we need if we express our vulnerability without first working on it inwardly. Only when we're aware of what our vulnerability entails, and what it wants from us, will we be comfortable with it. We need to first have a relationship with our *real self*. Once we have those answers, we'll feel more confident approaching people. If we are treated negatively, we'll not only know how to stand up for ourselves but that we should. If we don't follow this course, we risk being judged and treated poorly without having the tools to cope with it. This can make our situation rather worse.

Before we dive deep into the well of our soul, we must learn about vulnerability and its nature. Once we know more, we'll then be able to deal with any adverse consequences much better. The way people respond to what we have to share is based mostly on their experiences and the variables that played out in their own lives. We cannot blame them for this because that's the way they know it. This is why it's important to know what you're hoping to achieve before you share key information about your life. If your reasons are sound and it's the right thing to do, you must also know how to react if the conversation goes south.

So, what is a good reason? Our key purpose in making ourselves vulnerable is not to attain validation; it's to strengthen the bond we share with them. It's a great emotional task. Yet if we want to establish a relationship with ourselves where we know our triggers (what ticks us off, what makes us happy, what we don't wish to tolerate) we have to face who we often term as a "saboteur."

Vulnerability is not all that bad. It's overwhelming, yes. It's troubling. It's scary. But it's also a huge part of who we are as individuals. It's also the source of our perseverance, strength, patience, might, and resilience. Our vulnerability will be what we make it out to be—that's up without a down.

Our vulnerability allows us to become better versions of ourselves. It helps us learn the coping mechanisms that work best for us, and ones that drill us down even more. When we don't embrace vulnerability, we refuse to have solid conversations with people on topics that truly matter.

Vulnerability requires emotional exposure and a level of self-security that does not hinder our self-awareness. When you embrace awareness rather than fear it, you develop an understanding that makes life easier for you. Learning how and where to compartmentalize different emotions is an art well-learned through embracing vulnerability.

Compartmentalizing emotions in well-placed corners also helps us gravitate toward solutions in a much better scenario. We may get our emotions mixed up when we socialize in the same circle. For example, grief, anxiety, hurt, pain, loss, and frustration may camouflage in different forms. When we face these emotions head-on, decimating them for what they are, we achieve greater clarity and confidence.

Confidence bred from this particular exercise is what keeps us floating and maintains our sanity when we're vulnerable. It may seem like the vulnerability comes in blurting it on the outside, but internally it must follow a process if it is to succeed in its work. This is why we must not see the vulnerable as the bad guy or the good guy. Labeling it as one extreme or the other is not beneficial. Look at it exactly as it is: a medium that transpires to clarity, inner peace, confidence, and improved self-image.

Once we're comfortable with the idea of being uncomfortable with our emotions (or, plainly put, facing our emotions), we simultaneously tackle our fear of commitment.

The fear of commitment is essentially being afraid to dedicate ourselves to the maximum. Dedicating ourselves means giving it our all and, to a certain extent, exposing ourselves. That can feel tough, especially when we're not close to ourselves. A certain fright ensues when we're at the brink of exposing ourselves to people before we've first gathered the courage to come to terms with who we are. Commitment can extend beyond a relationship—it can be about a living place, a dream, a job, or other goals we've envisioned for ourselves. There's a fear of failing to succeed, to achieve our goal. Not knowing the outcome of our efforts can limit us from proceeding forward.

We don't want to commit because we're unsure if we'd want to be at that place six months from now, a year from now, or a decade from now. But that's the thing—we pressure ourselves to commit permanently. Yet our commitment does not have to be for life; it can also be restricted to just until we're not up for it anymore. As long as you're honest about your intentions with the people in question, you're good to go.

Thinking that we have to commit to something for our entire life can be anxiety inducing. But if you tell yourself that you can exit through the doorway if you feel it isn't right for you, then you're in a better place than you initially thought.

The fear of commitment partly stems from not knowing what the future may bring. Why commit to something you can't predict? We also stress about whether we are truly loyal, and if we're in it for the long haul. What we really feel negative about is having limited control over what may come. But that's the nature of every aspect of life! We can never know from day to day what the future will bring. Yet we don't stop living out of fear, so why should we stop committing? Intimacy issues can contribute to a fear of commitment. If not tackled, this problem can cause great distress for people, especially when they don't know how to start a conversation about it.

Intimacy issues usually follow avoidance that directly impacts the relationship, especially on an emotional level. We fear being emotionally intimate with our partner based on negative experiences in the past. We equate those experiences with relationships in general, and as a coping strategy, stay away from relationships as a whole. This seems safe to us; the danger is feels distant, not within reach. Intimacy issues may show up as low self-esteem, anger outbursts, avoidance of physical touch, trouble forming long-lasting relationships, unable to share personal details of our lives, inadequate sharing problems, or the lack thereof.

Childhood experiences play a defining role in intimacy issues. A lack of any or all of the abovementioned can create a sense of not knowing what love, care, or adoration is, and exposure to the greatest devil of them all: rejection.

Not wanting to commit has a long-standing relationship with rejection. By rejecting commitment, we protect ourselves from rejection, being 'thrown out.' We relieve ourselves from the worry of not being good enough and fulfilling someone's expectations. To avoid such anxiety-inducing thoughts, we exclude the mere option of them coming to fruition. As part of a safety mechanism, which didn't exist in childhood, we believe it's best to implement an arm's-length distance from all that can potentially harm us.

Unfortunately, the effects of avoiding intimacy and commitment are detrimental. While the short-term relief may outweigh any possible forthcoming damage, in the long run we find ourselves encompassed by the loneliness we slow-cook for ourselves. Effects of avoidance may range from, but are not limited to, social isolation, the risk of feeling depressed, and increased anxiety. Avoidance leads to short-term relationships defined only on the surface. If you walk down this path in life, you ultimately block the possibility of ever feeling truly happy. This all comes from believing that, since you never got it when you needed it most, you won't receive it now as well.

Compare variables and see if they still weigh the same. Remind yourself of the person you are today. The grief that is when such thoughts begin making sense to you, remind yourself of a time when you weren't provided love, care, and a safe preventing happiness in your life does not come from your current self but rather from your inner child. You are not that child anymore. Today, you have far more power, resilience, and knowledge of causes and their effects. Give yourself some credit for your growth since then. When you voice out your strengths, you allow them a chance to exist and fill the air. You will not suffer from negative consequences the same way you suffered as a child should you choose to resort to healthy coping mechanisms and effective strategies.

Going back into our shell is typically a regressive act, and while it may feel safe, it's only on the surface. Change takes place when you take charge and make the call.

2

Fear of Perfectionism

Fear of perfectionism, also called perfectionism syndrome, is the constant drive to make everything perfect. This fear is dangerous, as it encourages self-defeating behavior and thoughts. Unfortunately, it is a common fear since modern society pushes everyone toward the same kind of success. Constant critique and comparison make us feel worthless and hopeless.

These feelings of worthlessness and hopelessness don't let us stop. Instead, they only drive us to work harder and push ourselves as far as possible. While working hard and pushing ourselves are not harmful in themselves, doing so to the point of being overworked, burnt out, and exhausted is anything but ideal.

Perfectionism makes us compete with others in everything we do and promotes self-loathing if we are not constantly on top. It makes us forget that everyone has different skills and talents, which makes each of us unique. It also makes us forget that skills and talents can be improved. Instead, we want to be perfect before we even get started; to appear and act perfect, so we never fail.

More than anything, perfectionism makes us forget that it's not just us but everyone. Nobody is perfect at everything. In fact, nobody is perfect at anything. The most anyone can hope for is to be great, or the best, at something. There is no such thing as perfect.

I have struggled with the fear of perfectionism for twelve years. I spent those years trying to do everything perfectly. Eventually I let it all go, and I'm writing this to tell you and everyone else to do the same: let it go.

During those twelve years, there was no room for error in anything in my life. Everything had to be perfect. This included how I made my bed in the mornings, how my kitchen cabinets were organized, and how I worked. I would stay up all night to complete work assignments and projects. I would be working at home all those hours, and without pay. I did and redid my work just to make it perfect. I wouldn't allow myself to make mistakes. I'd barely allow myself to breathe!

At work, I would spend all my hours correcting the one thing someone pointed out that I did wrong. It would take everything out of me for anyone to correct my work. I would make sure everything was correct on Excel sheets and PowerPoint presentations. But perfecting everything didn't make me happy. Instead, it made me upset. I would be upset at myself for spending so much time on menial tasks. I would also be upset with my coworkers because I knew nobody cared about those things as much as I did. I would be bothered by their unbothered attitude. I would be bothered for them on every mistake they made while at work.

Now, years later, I can see I was suffering severely from perfectionism syndrome. It made me miserable. I was tired from all the hard work and investing time into things I didn't need. I was exhausted from feeling pressured to do it all perfectly. The burden of perfectionism was always on my shoulder, leading me to become upset at others for no reason.

For the longest time, I didn't even realize I was suffering from perfectionist syndrome because I believed all my expectations were realistic. I truly, absolutely believed I could be perfect. I didn't think I was chasing something unachievable. I didn't have the word *never* in my dictionary. Yet, ironically, everything started with the word never. Does this make sense?

I could never just do things poorly.

I could never allow someone to correct me.

I could never admit my own limitations as a human being.

I could never understand that not all tasks require absolute effort.

I could never admit that I didn't know something.

I could never utter, *"I don't know."* Even when I didn't know, I *had* to know it. I had to figure it out and learn and do it and do it *perfectly*.

Growing up, I was exposed to people who had the mindset that if you do something, you've got to do your best at it. This may sound like positive influence, but it caused me to become a perfectionist. This, in turn, did not allow me any room to acknowledge what skills or learning I was lacking. I just thought I had the answers intrinsically and didn't need help from others. I came to believe that uttering the words "I don't know" was wrong; I must know everything.

Perfectionism took root in my brain. Over time, the roots only spread, and the fear became stronger. Even when I was offered advice and mentorship, the fear of doing an inadequate job wouldn't go away. It would make me want to learn in an instant, to know it as soon as it was told to me and become better at it than the person who was teaching me.

I only realized I was suffering from perfectionism when I would repeat the task I had completed just to improve it. I would double- or triple-check it. At times, I would be so focused on the instructions that it would be difficult for me to actually follow them.

For example: If I was working on a project or assignment, and I received feedback about it, I would stay up until the project was perfect or I would start another one. I would even say out loud when I finished a project, or stare at it and say "perfect," and walk away. I didn't want to leave any room for errors.

It made me ask myself, *"Why am I doing this? What am I trying to achieve?"* These questions would pop up when I repeated a task so carefully that it would be poorly executed compared to the first time. When my second and third tries would look poorer by comparison, I would question why I felt so compelled to do it again when I had done it well the first time. I realized I was trying to perfect the minor details for no reason but to satisfy my internalized fear.

I know now that I wasn't alone. Many people describe themselves as perfectionists. They struggle to pursue their dreams because they don't want to fail at them. But failure isn't as bad as our society has made it out to be. Failure is a chance to learn where we lack then improve. It allows us a break to reflect on ourselves and our actions so we can try again with greater knowledge. We cannot be good at anything until we try it and fail at some point. Failure is essential for learning.

Perfectionism is the enemy of growth and creativity. It starts small, but it takes over your life. It builds a false idea in your mind of how things should be, and it forces you to do it the same way every time. Sure, there is a correct way to do everything, but it rarely involves looking at the finer details when the work output is only limited to ourselves. It makes us see everything the same way. We stop trusting and appreciating the uniqueness of the process. We don't care about learning and growth. In fact, as ironically as it sounds, perfectionism makes us resent learning and growth.

We often don't start a new career or join a gym because we want to be perfect at it before we even begin. We don't start the business because we want to make it an instant success. We don't create a website until we have acquired the best tools to make it happen. We will spend three days on something that doesn't even require forty-five minutes. We lose efficiency, creativity, and the ability to learn.

Fear of Making Mistakes

We get embarrassed when we think of sweating and panting in the gym. Similarly, we don't want to learn about the new career on the job, forgetting that it is impossible to master something without practice.

I wanted to create a fashion website. But I didn't do it for the longest time because I didn't own a Mac computer. I watched others create their fashion websites on Macs and believed I needed to do the same. I ignored the obvious fact that most of those I watched didn't have Macs when they began.

I wanted to create a fashion business, too, but I wanted to own a warehouse before starting. I also wanted to gain ten pounds, but I wanted to start consuming enough meals per day before I hit the gym. There were so many things I wanted to do that I didn't do because I wasn't ready to learn them. I only wanted to be perfect at them. I wanted to be perfect before I started them so I wouldn't make any mistakes. Perfectionism, for me, was a fear of making mistakes.

Our yearning to reach our destination can stand in the way of beginning our path. Our long-term goals may keep us from achieving the small milestones. For example, you don't have to own an expensive Canon camera to become a photographer. You can begin taking pictures on your cell phone and build your skill set until you can save enough money for that Canon. Without first polishing your skills and learning the science and art principles of photography, you wouldn't be able to capture good photographs from a professional camera, anyway.

Deconstructing Fear of Perfectionism

The fear of perfectionism comes from excitement. I was afraid to do my job poorly because I was thrilled to be there. I was overworking because I had a passion for working in the first place. But it was harmful to my work because it stopped me from actual professional growth. I did work harder than others and was rewarded for it. But I wasn't open to learning at all.

My struggle with perfectionism syndrome impacted my ability to learn. I didn't just spend all my time working and redoing all the work, but I also tried to come up with excuses for why my work was perfect even when I knew very well it wasn't. It became impossible for me to receive feedback. Since I was deprived of the necessary skill to always learn from others, I considered all feedback as criticism. I wouldn't allow others to tell me why my work wasn't how it should be.

At work, I would be the first one in and the last one out. I worked more than anyone else, so, of course, my fear told me that I knew better no matter what. To combat the criticism, I would work on a strategy in advance.

At home, I would complete the next day's work, then I would plan for making excuses as to why it was the best way to proceed. It was especially draining on my mental health because, even when I understood and acknowledged my lacking, I wasn't comfortable with the idea of looking like I didn't know something. I admitted to myself that I could not do everything perfectly, but the idea of admitting the same in front of others terrified me.

I struggled with this syndrome even more in my personal life than my professional life. I would spend hours and hours cleaning my home, steaming the sheets, and ensuring everything was color-coordinated. My home had to appear picture-perfect all the time. In short, the perfectionist syndrome had snatched my *comfort* from my own home. I wasn't resting at home; I was always working to prepare it to provide the perfect comfort which I never enjoyed.

If I wasn't satisfied with my own work, I would call my mom and ask her for her opinion. I would have her do a walk-through, and I would then repeat how she had instructed me to do something until I had perfected it. I wasn't just getting no rest at home; my health was also suffering because I wasn't eating much. I didn't want to order out because I wanted to eat healthily, but cooking is something I never enjoyed. Add to it the fear of perfectionism, and I wasn't going to eat something I cooked because it didn't look good on a plate or in a picture. I wanted to throw the food in the trash, and I have been guilty of wasting many delicious, fresh, and healthy meals because they didn't look the way I expected. I stopped cooking because I didn't like wasting food. I let the result stop me from even starting.

If I wasn't working, I was planning; if I wasn't planning, I was thinking of it. I also thought about things I had already completed so I could go back to them to make them perfect.

People always told me, "Teara, everything doesn't have to be perfect." I would always respond, "It's not perfect; it's an expectation."

Though I couldn't understand it at the time, I had to start telling myself that I had to let it go. Once I identified my deep-rooted perfectionism syndrome, I had to let things be. I knew I had to do it for myself, for my sanity, health, and peace. It had to stop before it took over my life and destroyed it. My life was meant to be peaceful for me. Yes, I had the distorted idea that I could only find peace in perfecting things, but that wasn't sustainable. I couldn't go on in life with this behavior set in stone.

I realized how my fear of perfectionism was holding me back from actually living my life. I realized that I couldn't spend my entire life repeating tasks at home and at work. I wanted to go out, spend time with my loved ones, create a new life with my significant other, and have new experiences. None of it could happen until I learned to let go of things that kept me occupied. My fear of perfectionism was holding me back from actually living my life.

When we get older, our priorities begin to change. Our definition of success changes, especially during our twenties and then during our forties. We have to balance the life we have created and the life we want to create. I could feel myself changing, becoming more conscious and intentional during my twenties. My wants and wishes were changing. I wanted different things at twenty-eight than I wanted at eighteen. To make room for these new experiences, I had to stop spending all my time, energy and focus on what didn't matter to me as much anymore. I had proved myself at work. I knew what I wanted to do in life. I didn't need to keep figuring it out or proving myself. I could enjoy the acknowledgement and appreciation I was receiving. I could allow myself the fruits of my labor.

I had spent days, weeks, and months barely eating, sleeping, working out, or taking care of myself in any sense because I had goals and dreams to meet. I wanted everything done before I allowed myself to enjoy it, but I wasn't stopping until I was done. I was trying to perfect it all, over and over, for no reason.

I wanted to allow myself the grace to slow down, to live in the moment. I knew everything didn't have to be perfect. But I had to come to terms with this fact and allow it to be my reality. The perfectionist syndrome was affecting my ability to enjoy my life. Even when I would find some time from all the work to enjoy myself, the experience had to be perfect.

Even when I was just spending time on my hobbies, they had to be perfect. If they weren't, I wouldn't feel satisfied or like I had enjoyed myself at all.

So, I made a promise to myself. I would prioritize my health and my mental peace. I would stop adding to my plate before I began eliminating. If I had any room to breathe between chores, I began doing exactly that: I breathed and relaxed. I had to clear my mind before I cleared repetitive tasks from my schedule.

As I moved on to the real work, I wrote three goals for anything I worked on:

1.   Work for two hours on the project.

2.   Have someone look it over and receive their feedback with an open mind.

3.   Breathe.

I would repeat these steps until the person advising me said the project didn't need any further changes. Then I made it a point not to work on that project any further. I would leave work at 5:30 pm and not work on professional projects at home. If I was working on a hobby or domestic chores, I decided the duration in advance and stopped no matter what.

I wanted to learn to take each task one at a time, so I could focus on improving rather than perfecting my work. I set reminders on my calendar to just breathe, and to *"make room for you; everything doesn't have to be perfect."* I won't say it wasn't difficult. Going to the gym was especially challenging. But once I kept following this strategy, I loosened up a little.

Perfectionism became pressure, and pressure became peace.

Through this process, I learned that the biggest challenge is to stop being in your mind. We have to unlearn our old habits to make room for new ones. There is so much life beyond perfectionism. Eat your breakfast without your laptop. Have conversations that have nothing to do with professional or personal projects.

In a way, I still struggle with it. It took me a year to quit all my perfectionist habits and pick up the ones that allowed me to live my life. For example, my perfectionist syndrome kicked in again when I started writing this book! I wrote and rewrote numerous drafts. I couldn't help it; it was like an obsession. I wanted everything in a certain way. I had to remind myself to finish it once before trying to make it better.

I can still hear my mom telling me to slow down, and that I should focus on the journey rather than rushing the process. I came to love the saying, *don't take the elevator; take the stairs.* The key is to keep walking rather than wishing you were already at the destination.

We talk a lot about setting healthy boundaries with others, but we don't talk enough about maintaining them with ourselves. Creating barriers for ourselves is essential to avoid getting lost in our minds. We need to listen to our gut, not just when being cautious about others but also when we are self-sabotaging.

Ever since I learned to let go of trying to perfect everything, I have grown as a person and a professional. Being a leader in a professional setting is not just about leading well but ensuring people's happiness. Coach and train, then let go. Trust your team just like you trust yourself.

Every day is different, and every day is difficult. But in the end, it will all be worth it. Don't try to control anything. I now challenge my team with a new goal every week. Trusting them to achieve it hasn't just proved to be the right decision, but it has helped me become more confident in my own ability. I look for character, attitude, and reliability; anything else can be trained.

Don't let your goals stand in the way of your journey. Get out of your head and into your reality. Recognize that starting small is the only way to achieve big things. If you already had big things, what would be the charm of pursuing them?

Everything doesn't have to be perfect, nor will it ever be. Accept the fact that "perfect" doesn't exist; then you can remind yourself that there's no point stressing about it. You can start wherever you are. You don't have to have everything. Reset, regroup, and recharge. Just strive to be better each day. Don't let the start stop you.

3

Fear of Disappointment

Fear of disappointment is the expectation of failing before making an effort. It is the expectation that we won't get what we want or what we are trying to achieve.

Fear of disappointment is harmful to all aspects of our life as it makes us disappointed in ourselves. It makes us think and believe negative things about ourselves. We neglect our talents and abilities and even our achievements in the past. We become our harshest critics.

While it is only natural, and even necessary, to strive to become our best selves every day, fear of disappointment negatively impacts our lives. We all hold high expectations of ourselves. We act, feel, think, and behave around others according to the standards we set for ourselves.

Thus, feeling disappointment in oneself can be extremely uncomfortable. It leads to sadness, anger, guilt, and annoyance. When we disappoint ourselves, our self-esteem takes a hit, and we lose our confidence.

Living with the fear of disappointment builds a negative, gloomy, and pessimistic view of ourselves and our lives. We stop enjoying the things we used to enjoy and doubt everything that makes us want to invest our time and energy. Left untreated, the fear of disappointment can snatch away all our happiness.

What Leads Us to Develop Fear of Disappointment?

We learn fear of disappointment from others because it always originates as a fear of disappointing someone else. It takes root in us from the constant or harsh criticism of our ideas, actions, appearance, or personality from someone we admire. It could be one or more people. For example, a parent's constant and insatiable desire to see their child succeed in everything they do may lead to expectations that child fears he or she cannot meet. Children also develop a fear of disappointment when they don't make friends at school easily. They may be different from the popular children in school and assume they would only be a disappointment to them, thus becoming disappointed in themselves.

As that child becomes a teenager then a young adult, they continue finding flaws in themselves. It is no secret that the teenage years can be severely emotionally challenging for many. At that tender age, children are trying to become too much while knowing too little about life or what they want from it. The lack of resources and support can worsen their fear of disappointment. Even children who perform well in the traditional schooling system can develop a fear of disappointment. The praise and attention they get for their hard work can make them afraid of losing it all. This may significantly damage their self-esteem as they learn to derive it from their achievements and not their values. They try their best to become *model* children who do everything right, leading them to develop a fear of disappointing others.

The fear of disappointment these children develop becomes stronger as they age. As adults, they shy away from being their own person or pursuing anything they want because they don't want to lose the praise or attention they enjoy. Their fear of disappointing others stops them from living their lives as they want to. It keeps them trapped in the same old traditions and routine, depriving their lives of any joy or excitement. With time, the fear of disappointing others takes root in them and wipes away any self-belief they may have. They begin to believe they cannot pursue anything they want, as failure would lead to negative consequences. For them, the stakes are high because failing means disappointing others as well as disappointing themselves.

While fear of disappointing oneself mostly originates from fear of disappointing others, it is usually felt more intensely. Fear of disappointing oneself always feels bigger than the situation. It sounds something like this: *If I don't get this, it means I am not good enough for it and don't deserve it.* This is called over-personalization of the fear of disappointment. It happens when we begin doubting our abilities and don't consider the many situational factors that played a role in our apparent failure. For example, if you apply for a job and don't hear back, it is easy to believe you never deserved it in the first place. However, chances are that the position was filled through a reference. It could even be that there were other applicants who could start earlier or were more suitable for the position. The greater suitability or higher qualification of other applicants has nothing to do with you, and it doesn't eliminate your achievements, qualifications, and suitability. Companies have meticulous hiring processes, and they like to hire a candidate that checks out on most, if not all, of their criteria.

Similarly, if your relationship doesn't work out despite your best efforts, it might simply be caused by a fear of commitment from the other person. If someone you find attractive doesn't reciprocate your feelings, they may be looking for something else in a partner or may not be over their ex. The point is that there are uncontrollable factors in any situation that play a part in determining its outcome. It's not about your worthiness in the situation or in any future situation. While your behavior always influences a situation one way or another, it isn't the only determining factor. So, it is important to realize that you can only do so much! Until we stop trying to separate our perceived reality from the actual reality, we will always be disappointed in ourselves. *Events are what we experience, not who we are.*

What Causes Our Disappointment?

Overcoming the fear of disappointment means no longer being disappointed in oneself. It doesn't mean we become proud of our flaws and stop trying to improve. It only communicates the idea that we accept ourselves as we are while trying our best. Overcoming this fear requires answering some tough questions, some of which are:

What should I do with my time and energy?

What traits do I have? What abilities do I have?

What are my values?

Why am I so afraid of disappointing people?

Be honest with yourself. You must also be ready to accept the difficult answers, swallow your pride, and confront yourself. It can be tough, given that you may already struggle with feelings of guilt, anger, and annoyance with yourself. But it is the only way for you to figure out who you are and what you stand for.

I won't tell you not to care about what others think. It is important to care about those we love and who want to bring out our best versions. But it is equally important that we value the same things for ourselves that others have for us and that our feelings align with them. For example, your parents may want you to become the best piano player of all time. But if you don't enjoy playing piano, or even music, it isn't something you should worry about or strive for. Similarly, if you want to achieve something only to gain the attention of those who you like but who don't like you back, you are only setting yourself up to live with a lifelong fear of disappointment.

You must also accept the fact that letting go of the fear of disappointment doesn't mean constantly letting people down. It is only about stopping the people-pleasing behavior that hurts you. It can be difficult to recognize this behavior. We often lie to ourselves and even believe these lies. This is why defining who you are and what you want is so important—so you can see through the lies you tell yourself. Ask yourself: *Do I enjoy the perks brought by doing what others want me to do?* Again, be honest. This is a judgment-free zone. You are only a human, flawed by nature. You are a product of your environment. If you answer *yes* to the above question, weigh the perks against those you can enjoy by pursuing your own path and doing what you are afraid to do.

Remember, it is your life. Only you can decide what you would enjoy more. If you choose not to give up on the perks you enjoy from doing what others want you to do, change how you think about it all.

You are not doing what you do out of fear of disappointing others. You are doing it because it brings you results you enjoy. If you believe the perks you enjoy from others are worth the hard work, think of them as your reward and not just perks. You have to work hard anyway, so if you choose to work towards something that brings certain results, there's no harm. It's simply a way to live an easy life. Life is hard, yes. But that doesn't mean we have to make it harder. If you can make the easy choice and find that it is worth giving up on some things, you have the right to do so.

However, this approach will make going after what you want even easier. Who says you have to do just one thing in life? You can do what others want you to do, enjoy the perks you get from it, and use them to pursue what you want. Make yourself happy while you also care for everyone else's happiness. But you must not make any of those choices out of fear of disappointment. You don't have to please people when they are not bringing you any happiness. You don't owe anyone anything, and neither does anyone owe anything to you. Any transaction that you choose to do with anyone must be done out of love and to increase the joy in your relationship with them. Moreover, like any transaction, it should always be fair to everyone involved.

This is especially important for those who develop a fear of disappointment during their early years. Since they fear disappointing others, they don't want to ask for help. As a result, they don't inform their parents when they need a break or when they cannot take it anymore. In school, these children may take up more than they can handle. The expectations built during their early years never stop or even slow down. Thus, they keep on fulfilling these expectations, and the fear of disappointment rooted in them grows deeper roots.

The fear of disappointing others becomes the fear of disappointing oneself in the same way. We internalize others' expectations of us and begin to see them as our own. In this way, when rooted in us early on, the fear of disappointment keeps us from exploring what we want from our life. It keeps us from forming our opinions and ideas. It prevents us from developing a unique personality. We begin to agree with those we don't want to disappoint every day. When we finally disagree, even on a minor issue, all that we had suppressed for years comes bursting out. Often, it creates a rift between us and those we have tried to please all our lives. Most parents become so used to their children being obedient that they begin to see them as mere extensions of themselves and not as individuals. Individuals who may have unique ideas, opinions, and feelings. When the first rift occurs, it often leads to one of two scenarios. Either it causes the then-grown child to suppress their feelings forever from fear of disappointing their parents ever again, or they let it all out in the wrong way, harming their relationship with their parents or maybe even cutting off all communication.

Since most of us develop the fear of disappointment from intentional or unintentional acts of our parents, it is important to remember that most parents wish their children well even when they are being too hard on them. These parents simply want to ensure a successful future for their children. However, they often forget that this successful future may not turn out to be happy.

So, after learning the distinction between what can help us secure a successful future and what will give us a happy future, it is up to us to inform our parents about it and seek their support. If they are not willing to extend their support, we can find partners and friends like family who will encourage us to pursue our happiness. However, it can only happen when we have the strength to break free from expectations and the courage to identify our fears. Of course, the fear of disappointment can make it challenging to bring up anything controversial, but we have to fight through it to emerge fearless.

I remember a time in my life when I had to be everything to everyone. I would help others more than I would help myself. I would never say no to anyone, even if saying yes killed me inside. I was always available for anyone who needed me, all while ignoring my own needs and wants. I answered every call, text, and email. I was a good friend, daughter, sister, mentor, counselor, and manager. I responded to everyone but my gut. I was everything but myself, and I was there for everyone except myself. I was losing myself in my effort to be there for everyone all the time.

I would never speak up for myself, and I let others make decisions for me. I would rather go to the beach than the mall, but I made countless mall trips because I could never say no. I would eat what others wanted and even pay for everyone's food if they just asked me once. Whenever anyone asked anything of me, my reply would be, "Sounds good" or "Okay."

Not being able to speak up for myself left me feeling constantly exhausted and frustrated. Many times I regretted not being able to say no, often immediately. I wanted to give myself a break, but I couldn't stop—until I couldn't take it anymore. I realized frustration is the same as disappointment. I was disappointing myself in the hopes of not disappointing others.

Like many others who deal with this fear, I didn't recognize it right away. However, I understood I was doing something wrong when I felt my boundaries were violated. I knew I wasn't setting them effectively, and I wasn't holding myself accountable to remind people of my boundaries. I realized I was afraid of saying no to people; I was giving in for fear of disappointing them. Moreover, I feared I was being unkind to people if I told them no, which meant that I was afraid of disappointing myself by not setting and holding up effective boundaries.

Needless to say, it happened too often. I would always oblige, whether it was meeting people when it was my time to unwind or going to the restaurant others wished. I compromised on everything, from how, when, and where I socialized to what salary I agreed upon at work. I understood I needed to be vocal about what I wanted and needed in any given situation and do it with grace. If I didn't, I would only continue feeling exhausted. I remember I opened the notes app on my phone and wrote that I would no longer be available for others. I knew my decision wasn't going to be easy. I knew how a lot of people had become dependent on my constant presence and were going to be hurt. But I couldn't keep exhausting myself. I was so tired of everything that I didn't want to do anything.

I knew what I wanted to say and how to lead a conversation where I wanted to reinstate my boundaries. But whenever it was time for execution, I wouldn't do it. I didn't want to hurt anyone's feelings, be labeled as opinionated or intimidating, or be viewed as unreliable. It was so difficult, because even though I knew that I was right and that I was worthy of being opinionated, I didn't want others to call me anything that wouldn't make me feel good. On the other hand, I knew those who truly cared about me would understand my decision and support it. They would be grateful for all I did for them and wouldn't mind if I couldn't do it anymore. I knew they wouldn't want me to exhaust myself for them, and that they wanted me to be happy with myself.

But it's not so simple. The truth is that we are not always ready for what we want. But this doesn't mean we shouldn't try. The process of trying can help us get ready if only we allow ourselves. We must learn to embrace disappointment as opportunities to learn instead of obstacles. We must empower ourselves to grow out of the fear.

It is essential because at one point or another, it gets to us. For example, a friend once asked me to help her redesign and re-organize her kid's room from 9:00 am to 5:00 pm on my day off. Saying yes to it meant missing out on my weekly self-care, going to the gym, treating myself to my favorite Mexican restaurant, and sitting in the park to read. Not that it mattered what I normally did; I would be sacrificing the one day of the week I got for myself. If I didn't utilize it as I pleased, I would be pushing myself to burnout. I decided to help and try to have the energy to do something for myself. Which I didn't have energy for myself.

So, you see, I have been there. I have sacrificed my needs for others to the point where my needs pile up and make it impossible for me to ignore them. Giving up an hour of extra sleep doesn't sound like much, but it is about getting enough rest to keep going. Now I have learned to tell others that I couldn't do more for them than I do for myself. I always calculate the cost of what agreeing to anything will take from my life, and only then will I decide if I want to do it. It is my response to friends, family, relationships, and even my work.

If you are also tired of feeling disappointed in yourself and getting over the fear of disappointment, you must stop and think about why you are doing this to yourself. Figure out yourself, discover what you want from life, find people who want you to be happy with yourself and your life, and start living life optimistically. Start saying no. Don't answer every call. Don't show up to everything. Work on yourself to improve instead of feeling disappointed in yourself. Don't waste your life and your time feeling guilty, angry, annoyed, or sad. No good will come of it. We are all imperfect; even those who you think are perfect are flawed human beings. Stop hating yourself. It won't make others love you. Identify your positive traits and your talents and nourish them. It's called a selfish season, but it's really a season of self-love.

I won't tell you it's easy. It took me years to overcome the fear of disappointment. We have to go through something to move past it, of course. We have to experience it, sit in it, and take action. I sat with myself learning to say *no* before I was able to speak up, create healthy boundaries, and say *no* to others.

The desire to improve and succeed in life shouldn't come with so many negative feelings. Enjoy your journey of trials, errors, failures, and lessons. It is easy to stretch yourself accidentally. People will try to make it happen. But you must stick to what you want and say it. *Do yourself a favor before you do it for anyone else.*

I now laugh when I tell my friends they are disappointed and upset not for disappointing others or themselves but for not being honest with how much they can handle. Helping others and being there for your loved ones is always important but helping oneself is everyone's primary duty. After all, we won't be able to help anyone if we don't take care of ourselves.

That's the purpose of getting over the fear of disappointment: to learn to value yourself. Be fearless in loving yourself and showing kindness to yourself.

Overcoming the Fear of Disappointment

Disappointment can be a touchy topic for many. Individuals may offer themselves up for self-sacrifice to avoid disappointing the people in their life, even if they're not attached to them or they don't hold an important role in their life.

For some odd reason, the fear of disappointing people hits differently because it leads us to believe that we're not incapable or even worthy of someone's time. Definitions of those expressing disappointment may be different from person to person. We often globalize our feelings pertaining to disappointment surrounding our life with it, but that's not how it has to be. Disappointment has a hand on us because of how we let it affect us. Our feelings and emotions are directly tied to what people think about us.

When we crave external validation, disappointment is bound to hurt us. Lessons in disappointment are a key takeaway for developing internal validation. You will continue to fear disappointment even if you aren't able to accept that you'll never be enough. We aim to be enough for the people in our life, but that's not the purpose of our time here. The perception people have of us has less to do with our output and more to do with how people perceive themselves and us.

Regardless of how much you may justify yourself, if someone does not want to see you in a certain light, you won't be able to change their mind. The idea that we can please everyone is a false concept. This ideology is neck-deep in seeking approval because we don't believe that what we give is enough or ever will be. Unless we don't set the narrative of what we can produce, and in honesty what we want to produce, we won't be able to attain the answers from anyone else.

The point here is that depending on external validation is dangerous and tempestuous. It can feel good to receive compliments and credibility from people because we naturally tend to believe external responses more than the ones we give ourselves. This is dangerous because external validation is lost along with the person when they leave your life. That leaves us looking for another place to get validation. It's a losing game. Moreover, we need to love ourselves enough to care about our own opinion more than what others think of us. The reason is that the way people treat us has less to do with how much they know us than the relationship they want to have with us and the boundaries they set. The way we treat ourselves has more to do with how well we know ourselves, how willing we are to discover ourselves, and how far we can go. This is stable ground to walk upon because our validation then looms over us. We're able to better justify how we feel about ourselves, and if it's negative, we also know how to re-route our mood to feel better. We don't have to rely on someone else's mood to feel better or drop our standards.

A steady ground helps with understanding ourselves better. If we do feel disappointed with our actions, it's something we can change. We may be tougher on ourselves, but if you want to succeed in life, you have to learn to rely on yourself and trust your instincts.

Learning how to cater to disappointment is a healthy start. Your response to action can be disappointing, and while on occasion, actions themselves can disappoint, it is your reaction that feeds how you feel. We cannot control everything in life, but we can control our reactions. They may be tough to target, but they're never out of reach. Develop emotional awareness to know what to do when you're disappointed. Start by letting it out, gaining some fresh perspective, and reflecting inward. It is important to come to terms with the situation, and if there are no reversible possibilities, then make peace with what has happened. Allowing a breeding ground for disappointment to form within can feel tumultuous, and it might throw you off your game more than you'd like it to.

Disappointment can be one of the most intense feelings that breed within us, so taking that power away from it is critical. You can do so by not allowing it to impact you more than it currently does. When we just let it sit, it compounds. It turns into a parasite that grows stronger every day.

When you're disappointed in someone, take a step back and realize that they're human. Treat them the way you would've wanted to be treated had you been in their place. Gain some perspective that will help you achieve self-clarity.

You'll also find a suitable way to balance variances when it comes to validation. When you're disappointed in someone, stepping back and gaining perspective will help because disappointment often projects itself in the form of an anger outburst. While we may instantaneously forget an outburst, those we took it out on can remember it for days.

Self-disappointment is a sign of your investment. The more you're disappointed and self-critical, the more passionate you are about the topic in question. When you align your purpose, goals, and output with your current situation, you'll find you're less upset. We set ourselves up for disappointment when we expect more than we need to. Dwelling on negative emotions can make us feel sad, forlorn, and unproductive. As the feelings rise in intensity, we may experience demotivation, suffering, and desolation.

One more factor to consider here is high expectations. The higher the threshold for our expectation, the more we're bound to feel disappointed. When we expect less, we naturally feel less affected. This can also happen when we set ourselves up for expectations without consulting the individual in question. A two-way street will lead to less havoc. However, when we anticipate and assume one's behavior to be a delight for something greater, that's when we invite hurt to take a seat.

4

Fear of Achievement

———❧———

Are you afraid of success? You may not know it, but there is a high chance you are. Perhaps you were told as a child that you would not be good enough or never amount to anything, etc.

Fear of achievement or success is more common than we realize. It is common to assume that everyone wants to be successful in their career, but the commonality of this assumption doesn't make it correct. The correct thing to assume is that almost everyone has the desire to be successful in their career. Many people do not have the desire to succeed in any aspect of life.

Those who have a fear of success don't believe they can do what it takes or that they are worthy of having what they want. This is fear of achievement. Fear of achievement is often confused with fear of perfectionism, fear of failure, or even fear of disappointment. But it is very different from all of them. The confusion occurs because it is not easy to understand any of the different kinds of fears. All fears spread their roots in our hearts and minds without us ever knowing. Even when faced with them, we are afraid to acknowledge their presence. We don't like to know we have been acting out of fear. We dislike the fact that we haven't had as much control over our thoughts and actions as we believed we did. If you have struggled with such confusion or feelings of denial, know that you are not alone and that it's okay to feel this way. It's all a part of the journey from fear to fearless.

As explained elsewhere in this book, fear of perfectionism is the fear of not being able to meet the impossibly high standards one has set for themselves. It eliminates room for error, learning, and growth. It requires everything to be perfect from the minute one sets their goals.

Fear of achievement, by contrast, is the concern that one will suffer as a consequence of reaching the goal they've set for themselves. This fear is more subtle than the fear of perfectionism. With fear of perfectionism, one is usually focused on the outcome of their goal when they set it. Thus, they are afraid to even start! The fear of achievement only shows up when we are nearing our goal. It's that, "OMG, I might actually succeed, what happens then?" feeling.

People also worry about what their friends and family will think if they become wealthy and successful. We might worry they will say, "What, you think you're too good for us now?" But really, they may be happy for us, and we are thinking of the worst possible scenario.

You find out who your true friends are when you are massively successful. Your true friends will be happy for you, and the others will stop talking to you.

Contrary to fear of perfectionism and fear of achievement, the fear of disappointing others keeps us from setting goals that only serve us. We're too busy worrying about how others will react. Additionally, fear of disappointing ourselves is like a self-fulfilling prophecy. It makes us disappointed in ourselves even when we have achieved success.

Fear of achievement and fear of failure can both keep us from reaching our full potential, yet they are two very different things. Fear of failure is beating yourself up when you think you have failed. Fear of achievement is the anticipation of what success will be like and how others will react to it. Each of these fears causes stumbling or failure to act. Fear of success, on the other hand, may not sound like much of a fear, but it is very real, and it can also hold you back in a big way. Mostly, it is your own behind-the-scenes manipulations that keep tripping you up on the road to success. In other words, when you fear success, you may unconsciously (or even consciously) cause yourself to fail.

What Leads to Fear of Achievement?

Many people are not aware they have a fear of achievement. Still others, after being presented with the proof, remain in denial. After all, fear of achievement can be hidden behind wishes, wants, and needs.

We all believe that it's safe for us to win. We believe that we deserve every bit of happiness we want. Success brings many good things with it. It brings freedom of time, the ability to buy a house and car of our choice, resources to go on exotic vacations, and so on. On the surface, it can appear as if everyone wants it all, leading to the incorrect assumption that everyone wants success.

So, why would anyone fear success when it comes with so many good things? Why would they develop a fear of achievement when it is meant to change their lives for good? Here's the answer in a nutshell: everything has a price, including success. That price can feel prohibitive. We know that when we achieve something we will also lose something. What we lose can differ, but there is no doubt we will have to give something up in order to gain something else.

For most, success can mean leaving their comfort zone. Success means gaining something new, which means change. Change in how we think, feel, and see things, in the way we respond and do things, and in our very lives. This change can be challenging. Despite our desire to achieve, the fear of consequential and inevitable change keeps us from trying to achieve it.

My struggle with fear of success wasn't too different. I would worry unnecessarily about imaginary consequences if I achieved success. It made me second guess myself and my goals. Some days I overanalyzed everything to the point that I was unable to sleep. I was so preoccupied with my fear that I couldn't even focus on my goals. I was scared of what success might cause me to lose, what compromises I would have to make, and so on.

For example, I wanted to gain ten pounds, but I was unsure if it was too little or too much. I was worried I might not like how I looked. I was afraid my favorite clothes wouldn't fit me anymore. I was overwhelmed with the thought of making time and curating a whole new wardrobe. I wanted to be successful, but I was also scared of what it might bring, as well as what I might have to give up in achieving it. It was a paradox. All fears are a paradox, really. They don't make any sense, but they are as real as any of our other emotions.

I knew I was suffering from a different kind of fear. I had already overcome a few, but this was new to me. Though I had reached a point where I didn't have a problem with looking in the mirror and acknowledging my struggle, I still lacked the motivation to overcome yet another fear. Some days it felt exhausting. I was trying to constantly walk away from my comfort zone. I was constantly struggling against the fears that had become part of my personality, my thoughts, and my instincts. It wasn't easy. There were many days when I wished I didn't care about achieving more in life. I wished I didn't have all these wants and wishes and could be happy with a mediocre, ordinary life.

I was faced with a difficult choice. On the one hand, I was afraid, but I had the comforts of familiarity, even if they were limited. On the other, I wanted to create a better life for myself, but it could only happen if I were ready to give up the comforts I had. The truth is, I doubted myself. I wasn't sure if I had what was required to achieve my goals; I had a fear of achievement. But I knew what I had to do. As I had before, I wrote it all out. I mapped a plan to follow so I could feel pumped with motivation. Yet I still reached the conclusion that I couldn't do it. I was still indulging in negative self-talk. It made me wonder, *Am I scared of getting over all my fears?*

This realization helped me analyze how bad my case of fear of achievement was. It was acting as the root of multiple fears I believed I had overcome. I needed to start all over again despite the progress I had made. I remembered the advice my pastor had always given me: "Success comes in pieces, not chunks, but it's up to you to find the pieces." I knew I wanted more from life, so I had to be okay with collecting the pieces as I found them.

Fear of change is one of the most common reasons we allow fear of success to hold us back. As humans, we thrive on routine and tend to fear uncertainty. While most of our natural fears help us survive in this unpredictable world, the problem is that change is the only constant. It isn't really a problem, but that is how we see it. Moreover, we don't admit to being scared of success because we all believe we want our lives to change for the better. But while it may be true that we want our lives to change, we can sometimes hesitate when it is in our capacity to make change happen. We want it until we can have it. When we find it's within our approach, we don't find it necessary or even desirable.

In some cases, it makes sense. Success can bring changes that are sometimes social in nature, meaning that you might lose someone worth sharing it with. This change is truly scary. But it is part of the journey. Yes, you will lose those who you love and cherish, but you will also find new people who will be happy in your happiness. People who will contribute to your wellbeing by cheering on your efforts rather than holding you back.

The change achieving success brings will not only transform your life, but it will also transform you. Once you have achieved success, you may realize that you don't want the people who held you back and couldn't celebrate your happiness. You will understand that those who wanted you to hide your talents just so theirs could shine were not your well-wishers. You will also acknowledge that you don't want to spend your life with those who have no more desire to improve their lives than yours.

When you lose people, you will have to give up on your feelings for them. You also must let go of many memories and sentimental items. It may feel overwhelming, but that's also part of the journey. Success is overwhelming. It brings immense joy, greater freedom, and new experiences. If you want to feel overwhelming happiness, you will have to go through similar levels of discomfort. However, there is one thing that you will never have to give up and that is trying to reach success. Your constant and consistent effort is what will get you there.

Another factor that contributes to fear of achievement is our appreciation of struggle. Society tends to respect those who struggle to achieve what they own more than those who get it easily. This is probably a good thing. But it is society's distrust and resentment towards those who don't appear to struggle that makes us fear success.

People like to share their problems with each other. When someone whines about how tough their job is, you are supposed to agree and share your everyday struggles. We know how unpleasant we may appear if someone complains about their life, and we respond by talking about how blessed we feel. We may come across as mean and inhumane, even when we are just sharing how we feel. Instead, we have to share the bad things about our life and the hurdles we faced on our path to success. Though not intended, participating in this social norm keeps us focused on whatever wrong is happening in our lives. This practice keeps us fixed in a place where we don't want things to improve, and we eventually develop a fear of success.

Nobody wants to be the odd one out. We all want to fit in with those around us. We don't want to be labelled a buzzkill, appear demeaning toward our friends, or act like a snob. We can especially come across as mean or cruel if we express the idea that we are better than those around us. That can lead to our relationships failing.

Even if we get over our hurdles, we cannot share the happiness of progressing on our journey with others. We cannot share obstacles we came across in the past. If we do that, we are reminded of how easy things used to be. We are termed *lucky*. Those who are still struggling, probably due to their many fears, tell us that we cannot relate to them and that we can never understand their struggles. Since we got over the hurdles and they didn't, they assume that our hurdles were easier. All our struggle and hard work over the years is immediately forgotten. We become privileged. Nobody wants to believe we are self-made because it makes them feel as if they aren't trying hard enough, which isn't true.

Achieving any goal requires effort. Nothing comes easy in life.

People often see someone successful and think that person just started doing that thing or was an overnight success, but that person has probably been working hard at it for 10-20 years, seeing very little success until now.

Most people will quit rather than keep working for years and not seeing much success until years down the road.

No profession or lifestyle is more challenging than the other. Everyone faces unique struggles that we can never know until we step in their shoes. But we can never step in anyone's shoes because, if we do, who will walk in ours?

So, it is no surprise that fear of achievement often arises from fear of being perceived in a wrong way. We want to keep struggling because we want to stay victims. The title of *winner* is scary. It is isolating and lonely.

When someone shares a story with me, I have noticed that I sometimes respond by sharing a similar experience of my own. My intention is to relate and connect, but I've come to realize that it can sometimes be perceived as me trying to overshadow their story or suggest that my experience was better or worse.

We want to stay relatable. This is especially true for the times we live in today. It has now become a trend, almost a game, for people to find something to be offended about or to turn themselves into victims. Of course, I don't mean to disregard anyone's experience, but I believe we can sometimes disregard real struggle while touting our comparatively small issues. We do so because we want to be the ones who can relate to others the most. We want others to believe that we are working hard, harder than everyone else.

One of the most sought-after results of success is recognition, but achieving success doesn't always bring it. Instead, it only comes during our struggle, so we always want to keep struggling, fearing the common outcome of achieving our goals: being labeled as someone who has it easy. The question is, why are we so ashamed of completing our journey? It is baffling how achieving success has become a source of shame and guilt for people. No wonder we all want to stay and be perceived as victims. As mentioned earlier, there is another label that can haunt us once we accomplish our goals, and that is being better than others. This label can be even more isolating. It outcasts us from those we have known all our lives. It turns our vulnerable moments where we share our struggle with others into boasting or bragging. Yet achieving success doesn't free one's life from further struggles. In fact, every stage of life brings its own issues.

Maintaining success can also be more challenging for some than achieving it. Nevertheless, those who struggle alongside us but don't achieve their goals as we achieve ours don't acknowledge this. Our struggles to maintain success sound like fake news to them. They perceive us as self-pitying victims who don't want anyone to see their happiness. This misperception can leave us not only feeling alone but misunderstood and betrayed.

It can be challenging to navigate how to show your real struggle and not just appear as a victim while sabotaging your own success. Maybe that's because society decides who can be a victim while continuously changing the definition of victim. Victimhood may earn us easy relatability to others, but it is important to remember that achieving success also earns us a relatability—one that is more lasting and impactful.

Do we want to relate to those who are too afraid to improve their lives or complain without trying? Or do we want to relate to the achievers? The choice is ours.

How to Overcome Fear of Achievement

It doesn't sound easy; that's because it's not. But from my personal experience, let me tell you that it is worth it.

My life was never the same once I understood that it's okay to be successful. I never liked standing out, and I didn't want others to think I was better than them because of all   I had accomplished. But I realized that I wasn't benefitting myself or anyone else by hiding my skills and abilities. Instead, I was keeping myself and others from benefiting from what I had to offer.

Once I realized how I was, in fact, actively withholding myself from doing good for myself and others, I started asking myself why I was so afraid of succeeding. I came up with several potential answers. They were all correct to some extent, and altogether, they developed and strengthened the fear of achievement inside me.

Setting Low Goals

Keeping the bar low can keep us from feeling challenged enough to strive for it. When the goal doesn't excite us, it is only natural not to care about it. It is both a cause and consequence of fear of achievement, turning our lives into mediocre, vicious cycles.

Avoiding Backlash

This is a common reason for fear of achievement. Even when we do want success, our apprehension of people's reactions can make us give up on it. This reason can especially lead to fear of success when our definition of success differs from that of people near and dear to us. This reason becomes stronger if those around us don't want to succeed in life in the first place. We fear setting and achieving goals as we don't want to become the odd one out.

Attracting Attention

Even those of us who appear confident can have their doubts. Success often brings increased attention, which can be unwanted by many if we are simply not social enough. The increased attention can also bring expectations from others, which can instill doubt in our ability to live up to them. Since the attention we get is more likely to be negative, resulting in others misunderstanding and alienating us, it can play a significant role in keeping us from achieving our goals.

Persisting Health Issues

Another common reason people develop fear of achievement is health issues. Mental health problems such as anxiety are more likely to make one not want to do more even to achieve their goals. However, physical health issues may often make success appear overwhelming and demanding. While they appear as valid reasons, as one must always prioritize their health, giving up on life goals for health issues isn't the solution either. Instead, better health must take priority over most other goals.

Giving in to Gender Stereotypes

Giving in to gender stereotypes is a common reason for women and other minority gender groups to be afraid of success. Though I had earned my position as the manager of the store I worked at after years of hard work, I did struggle with believing I truly deserved it, at least in the beginning years.

As a woman, I worked here for years and always wanted to keep elevating. Being great at my job always stopped right before I became executive or vice president.

After all, it isn't uncommon in our society to diminish women's achievements. No matter what role a woman wants to assume in her life, she is never good enough. Women are also made to feel less feminine when they succeed in the corporate world or any of the male-dominated industries. Hence, many women give into these stereotypes and stay away from accomplishing anything that can bring their womanhood under criticism.

Imposter Syndrome

It is a shame that imposter syndrome affects the smart ones, as they can achieve all their goals with less difficulty otherwise. Those suffering from imposter syndrome never believe themselves to be deserving of success and, hence, fear achieving it. And that's not all. These people sabotage their life the most as they feel like villains in their own stories. They often feel like they are fooling people and that one day everyone will see their (self-perceived) truth and they will lose it all. Thus, they don't pursue any of their goals and spend life held back by the fear of achievement.

Fear of success seems like such a strange concept. Why would anyone be afraid of their own success? I mean, isn't it what we are all hoping for, anyway—having all our wildest dreams come true? What else could be better?

The first step toward overcoming the fear of achievement is realizing how strange it is. The second is realizing that success comes with a lot of baggage. Becoming successful in any aspect can mean more public exposure, greater responsibilities, and heightened pressure, both from yourself and others. But that's just how it is, no way around it. This is the price of achieving your goals. If the fear of achievement is keeping you from the life you want, you have to become okay with paying the price of success. Trust me, it will be for the better.

In my experience, the fear of achievement is an overshadowing condition that is caused by various underlying factors. The culmination of these factors leads to a fear of success. In simple words, we are not afraid of achieving our goals, but we are afraid of its side effects. There's only one way to overcome it, which is to know that failure is not an option. I say this in two ways. First, you have to keep trying when you mess up. No matter how big you mess up or how badly you fall apart, you cannot give up. It is simply not an option for you. Second, I believe failure does not exist on the path to success. The path to success always remains the path to success.

It becomes a failure only when we give up and walk away. Remember: you aren't failing when you are falling. You are still on the journey. Falling is just part of that journey. Get up, dust yourself off, and continue on.

Another way of saying this is that progress is achieved through trial and error. No great inventor or scientist ever achieved their goal without failing along the way. Thomas Edison failed constantly. Einstein spent years trying to work out the math to prove his theories on relativity. Focus on what every hurdle in your path teaches you. Learn the lesson it wants to teach, so it becomes easier for you to overcome the obstacles you will face ahead. It is a part of your journey. No path is without bumps, turns, and stops. Once you acknowledge this truth and get comfortable with it, you will be able to walk on the path with greater confidence and patience.

Every challenge you face on the path to your goals is an opportunity to draw conclusions and learn lessons that will help you quicken your pace toward your goal. It is the chance to make adjustments, improve skills, ask for advice, and wait for the right moment to jump ahead. We all have to look for directions when visiting a new place. Whether we ask a person or open the GPS in our phones, it doesn't matter. Don't hesitate or feel ashamed to seek guidance. Reading this book is one way to do it. Above all, don't care what others think of you when you fall or feel stuck because of the hurdles on your path. Those who don't care about you won't approve of you whether you are failing or succeeding.

The thing that worked for me was resetting my mind. I told myself I would only focus on going to the gym every day instead of reaching my weight goal. I focused on eating nutritious food instead of eating more. I learned that I had to focus on one thing at a time and leave the consequences to when they present themselves. I couldn't let the fear of what might come overwhelm me to get to where I wanted to be. I knew that if I could cross all the hurdles to reach my goal, I could handle anything that came with it.

I had to do it. That's the point I had reached in my life. I needed to. I couldn't continue living with a fear of achievement along with all the other fears. I told myself, *"Feel the fear and do it anyway."* It became my mantra. I started showing up for myself.

I changed my goals, too. The new goals were much simpler: speak positively to yourself, don't complain to anyone, take one day at a time, and start taking responsibility for yourself. These goals paved the way for other actions I wanted to include in my daily life. I still couldn't tell myself, *"I can do it,"* but I had begun telling myself, *"I have to do it."*

Each day I gave myself instructions to follow. The steps were carefully broken down day by day to achieve a larger goal. Planning ahead was essential to ensure success.

It worked. It was easier to overcome the fear of achievement when focusing on the now. I know it doesn't sound easy. Most people live either in the past or the future. But living in the present isn't impossible. It is much easier on the mind when you get used to it. Try it; I promise you it will change your life for the better.

On the flip side, I believe a person cannot improve themselves when they aren't ready to acknowledge they have a problem. You must be honest with yourself. It is also important not to dwell on regret. Don't try to change your life from the past. Work on the present. Don't miss out on the lessons that brought you here that can still take you so much farther in your journey.

Every moment on the path to success takes place for a reason. It is all-important. It will all add up. Don't try to erase it, and don't compare your journey with others' journeys. Everyone's story is different. I say my overnight success took ten years, and I only look back at it with fondness. I can see my own growth. What can be better than that?

It is a pleasure to be able to grow, flourish, and thrive through the hurdles. Fear of achievement is just another hurdle on the path to achieving your goals. You can get over it just as you get over other obstacles.

It is easy to act on fear of success by quitting.

Quitting on the verge of success is blatant proof of fear of achievement. Our fear encourages us to find a reason to quit. The reasons for quitting can be varied, but the temptation can be equally high, no matter the circumstances.

I overcame my fear of achievement by disallowing myself to quit. I made it a rule: I will not quit what I set out to achieve. It didn't matter if I realized it wasn't going to do much for my life or if I changed my decision about it. My advice to you is the same: do not give up. It doesn't matter what your reason for developing and acting on fear of achievement is. You can eliminate the fear by simply not giving up. Repetition allows us to get used to things. Repetitively achieving success will help us get used to it and overcome the fear. So, go ahead and achieve whatever little or big goals you have.

We cannot make a change in our lives until we acknowledge to ourselves that the change is in fact necessary. We must have insight into our true selves to achieve honesty with ourselves. This insight is also essential in allowing us to know the ways in which our fear of success stops us or makes us sabotage our progress. Personally, I found it helpful to analyze the past instances when I did achieve success. I tried to remember my thoughts and feelings during those times and compared the ones stemming from my fear. Exploring how I went from fear to fearless helped me map out my journey to go where I had once been.

The journey from fear to fearless wasn't easy. It included answering some tough questions, but this exercise allowed me to see exactly when and at what points along my journey I would develop fear of success. The questions included:

- Are there distinct patterns to when I achieve goals and when I don't?
- Are there any traumatic instances that played a role in my approach toward my goals?

Answering these questions allowed me to get to the root of my fear and figure out when it took place inside me. Getting to know my fear and myself, inside out, allowed me to counter the negative thoughts and feelings it gave me. I began separating myself from the fear. I would differentiate between what I wanted to do and what the fear wanted me to do which helped me strengthen my belief in the actions I wanted to take. The practice wasn't too different from saying affirmations out loud and motivating oneself. I know a lot of people don't believe in positive self-talk or affirmations. We want others to validate our beliefs and actions. But nobody can match the energy and conviction with which we can encourage ourselves and change our mindset.

Only we can change our own lives. It begins with identifying the need for change and deciding on a destination. It progresses through mapping a course of action and ends with executing the plan. This doesn't mean that motivational videos or self-help books don't help. It simply means that, while others can help you realize the change needed in your life and give you strength to make that change, it is ultimately your decision to implement anything in your life.

If you find it awkward to engage in positive self-talk, you may take up journaling instead. In many ways, writing down our thoughts and feelings is even more helpful than saying them out loud. Writing helps release the intense emotions we feel onto the paper where we can make sense of them. It also helps us let go of negative thoughts and feelings and makes room in our mind for new and positive ideas. Not to mention journaling feels more private if you don't want to share your emotions or affirmations out loud, even if you only have bare walls around you. You don't have to restrict yourself to getting rid of negative thoughts and reinforcing positive ones, either. You can utilize the practice to explore what you want or don't want in your life and how these desires fit into the life you want to create for yourself.

Unfortunately, the practice of journaling isn't as popular as it once used to be, but trust me when I tell you it was popular because it deserved to be. Daily journaling allows us to keep a track of the events that take place in our lives and makes it easier to look back and analyze where things began to change. Writing down things when they are fresh also improves our ability to remember them in the long term. It makes us reflect on events and process our emotions regarding them as they happen, allowing us to stay on top of and in control of them rather than letting them pile up and undermine our logical and rational side.

If you take up this practice, make sure you write the happy and positive events that take place in your life each day. They don't really have to be events. They can even be instances, like a compliment from your boss over a project well done, a note of appreciation from a friend or family member, etc.

Negative thinking patterns aren't developed in one day. While certain traumatic situations can have an intense impact on our thought pattern, it is usually a slow and steady process. Yet humans are resilient. We have survived years of natural disasters and wars and diseases, yet we continue to strive for a better future for ourselves and coming generations. As those living in the most advanced and informed times, we must be grateful for being able to share our struggles and their solutions with each other and make use of the resources available to us to improve our lives in various aspects.

Success isn't as scary as you might think. It is a measure of growth. Anytime you stop growing, it is your fear of achievement telling you, *"Don't do it."* Don't listen to that voice! It might sound like you, but it is only the fear trying to hold you back. Move ahead and you will silence it.

They say, "You win some, you lose some." It's true. You *will* lose some. It can't be helped. But you will also win, and what you win will be much better than what you lose.

5

Fear of Growth

Fear of growth is the fear of outgrowing others. While it sounds like a good thing, it can be extremely uncomfortable, simply because it can be isolating and downright lonely.

But we can only become better by improving more than others. If we only improve as much as others, it wouldn't lead us anywhere special. In fact, when others improve further, they will leave us behind once more.

Sometimes we believe we are stepping outside our comfort zone when we are not. We believe we are making progress when we are only keeping up with those around us. It is no secret that success lies beyond our comfort zone, which is often dependent on those around us.

For example, if most of your high school classmates went to college, going to college wouldn't feel scary. But if you were the only person in your class planning to go to college after high school, it would seem like a bigger goal. In the former scenario, you may believe you are achieving a personal goal, but you are not. You are merely keeping up with those around you to prevent social outcasting. You may fear growth in this scenario, too, but it won't be evident.

It is common for fear of growth to go undetected as people in our surroundings are usually motivated to improve their lives. We follow our goals as others follow theirs, sometimes without even consciously pursuing them. For a lot of people, going to college or getting a promotion at work isn't even a goal but a natural progression they know will occur. These people are likely to suffer from fear of disappointment in addition to fear of growth, as they don't want to be the ones left behind while everyone else around them moves forward.

However, people suffering from fear of growth don't want to move ahead and lead the way for others, either. In simple words, this fear makes one want to stay in their comfort zone at all times, which shifts according to the people in their surroundings.

Fear of growth can sound similar to fear of achievement. However, fear of achievement stems from the uncertain consequences it may bring, while fear of growth stems from outgrowing others around you. While both fears stem from the unknown, the factors vary. With fear of achievement, the uncertainty lies in consequences. With fear of growth, it lies in stepping outside one's comfort zone.

How Fear of Growth Stops Us from Living

Like any other fear, fear of growth can prove significantly harmful if allowed to persist, deepen, and strengthen. It not only limits our progress, but it makes us dependent on others in the worst ways possible. It makes us feel uncomfortable pursuing anything new which hasn't been pursued and achieved by someone else in our surroundings. In this way, it makes us give up on our interests and passions. We become afraid of taking risks and exploring things unknown to us.

Fear of growth makes us live a safe life in our comfort zone. This safe life may be less stressful, but it is also less joyful. The fear keeps us from discovering our natural talents and turning them into skills. Thus, it prevents us from living a better, fuller, more content life—feeling more alive. It turns our life into mere existence.

I will say it again: life begins outside the comfort zone. So, if you want to live your life, you must stop fearing growth. Everyone has their own life to live; you cannot wait for others to progress in their lives before you allow yourself to move ahead in yours. You don't need anyone's permission; neither are you anyone's responsibility. You are responsible for extending your comfort zone by constantly improving your life. Go learn something new, achieve greater than what you have already, make your dreams a reality, and leave behind a legacy. To do this you must overcome your fear of growth.

How do you do that? By being uncomfortable. It is important not to shy away from doing things that you know will make you feel this way. It may be challenging, but it's the key to growth.

How to Be Uncomfortable

To become uncomfortable successfully and turn that discomfort into growth, list everything that holds you back from going after what you want. It doesn't matter if anyone you know has done those things before. Once your list is ready, identify one of the factors you can challenge. Repeat this activity every day. Every morning, make a list of your discomforts. Then at any given time during the day, attempt one of the actions on the list. Try to challenge a new factor each day, so it doesn't get too overwhelming, and you can experience different kinds of discomfort. You may find that some are worse than you expected them to be, but you may also find that some aren't as bad as you thought.

Gradually, try to spend more time being uncomfortable each day. You can also experience the discomfort more intensely as your tolerance builds for it. Try attempting two uncomfortable actions together or one after the other to make the exercise more challenging for yourself.

One of my favorite examples of growth is that of military personnel. I grew up in a military family, so I got to see this firsthand. Like other military families, we moved around a lot as my father was assigned new posts and jobs. Military personnel who make it a career serve in multiple ways throughout their career. This may sound like the worst thing about the military, but it it's actually a good thing in a way, as they are constantly pushed out of their comfort zone. As soon as they settle into one position they tend to get promoted to greater responsibilities. As they grow used to one department, they are sent to serve another. Their departments, positions, and locations can change as often as once a year, encouraging them to learn something new all the time. They not only become capable of surviving in extreme conditions but also become highly adaptable to every situation.

Of course, this doesn't mean that they stop being uncomfortable after a while or get over their fears completely. Humans   fight through their unique personal challenges and fears whenever   they are pushed out of their comfort zone. Not to mention new and strange things can seem fearful even when they are not. But the capacity of military personnel to overcome challenges and prove themselves over and over again allows them to experience real growth.

In my opinion based on personal observation, there are five steps to growth:

1. Recognize and Embrace Discomfort

Growth occurs only when we step outside our comfort zone. To grow, we must embrace the fact that it isn't possible to grow without discomfort and that embracing discomfort isn't possible without acknowledging it. We often don't want to acknowledge that we don't like being uncomfortable. We want to believe we are braver and stronger than we are, sometimes for ourselves, and other times for other people. In both cases, we stay in denial. Through denial, we limit the possibility of our growth.

Acknowledging the discomfort is the first step to embracing it. Keep reminding yourself that feeling uncomfortable is a natural part of the growth process. You only feel discomfort when you challenge yourself, when you want to be somewhere other than where you are. For example, military personnel know that moving constantly is a demand of their job. They cannot opt out from it. It is a natural part of being a part of the force.

2. Take Small Steps

Our fears are often stronger than we anticipate, but we don't have to overcome them in one big step. Start small. Push outside the comfort zone only slightly. You don't have to take one big step, just cross the boundary even if you only put half of your foot outside.

Be gentle and patient with yourself. It's not a task, it's a journey. You can take your time. You are not answerable to anyone but yourself. Try to achieve something that requires going only slightly beyond your current capabilities. Gradually increasing the difficulty of your goals will help build your confidence, making bigger growth opportunities appear less daunting. The saying, "Small and steady wins the race," sounds cliché, but it is cliché for a reason, that reason being it's true. Consistent effort, even if small, creates better and lasting results than quick, hurried, inconsistent efforts.

3. Celebrate Your Progress

Don't downplay your efforts. Celebrate every win, even if it's half a step outside your comfort zone. Recognizing your progress is as important as acknowledging the discomfort and the fear.

You may be tempted to compare yourself and your progress with others at this point. Don't do it. If you do it unconsciously, don't let it get to you. Check yourself before you disregard your progress. You may have been looking up to others to check possibilities in your life, but you are outgrowing that behavior. You are outgrowing who you were.

We celebrate birthdays, which is nothing but growth in years. Why can't we celebrate growing emotionally and in life? Pat your own back. You will be amazed at the motivation it brings you.

4. Seek Support

Seeking help from others in the form of guidance and encouragement is different from looking up to them. However, it is important to realize that you won't get support from everyone. Unfortunately, not everyone in your life will be able to see you thrive. But fortunately, there will be many who will be happy to encourage and guide you on this journey. It may take some time, like everything in life does, but you will find your support group.

Make friends with people who have overcome their own fears. Find mentors or professionals who have pushed the boundaries of their comfort zones and achieved big goals. Build your network, take encouragement from them, and offer the same when they need it, so you and every member of your network can grow.

5. Reframe Failure as Learning

Failure can be demotivating for anyone. But for those suffering from a fear of growth, it can be an especially negative experience. Upon taking a step out of your comfort zone, you may find yourself fallen on the path or a push against you forcing you back inside. But you must understand that this is how it's going to be.

Every setback and failure is an opportunity to learn and improve. You are growing; you will suffer from growing pains. But, eventually, you will be stronger for it.

Don't be disheartened and don't give up. Be patient with yourself. Rest when you feel the pain. Allow it to subside before you move forward. During this period of rest and healing learn the lesson life is trying to teach you. You must also learn how to navigate the world outside your comfort zone so you can reach your destination, your goals. Learn your lessons and take steps at your own pace. With perseverance, patience, and willingness to step outside your comfort zone, you can overcome your fear and embrace your personal growth.

Here's a fact: the more you feel fear, the more you grow. When you don't feel any fear, it indicates you are sitting in your comfort zone, surrounded by safety and certainty. The greater your fear and discomfort are, the farther you are from your comfort zone. It is only when you experience discomfort that you can be sure you are growing. While you can never   get used to being uncomfortable, your capacity to tolerate it will strengthen the more you are exposed to it. After all, fear is the ultimate indicator of growth. By achieving your goals outside your comfort zone, you can expand them from your starting point to your destination.

As mentioned elsewhere in this book, fear is actually a good thing. However, it is simply one emotion among many, and it should not cause us to lose our way. It ensures our survival by allowing us to sense danger. Every emotion, when felt, processed, and utilized, can significantly improve our life. Yes, it is uncomfortable to be afraid, but by allowing yourself to feel fear, you can sense which direction to take for a better life.

A person who fears is a person who dreams. Without dreams and goals for a better tomorrow, there would be no reason for us to fear anything.

Fear of growth is often fueled by assumed limitations. People who fear growth think, "What if?" instead of "How can I?" They set barriers for themselves on the path to their destination. They halt their progress even before they set out on their journey. Because of these limitations, they find refuge in their small comfort zone instead of expanding it.

As I mentioned, the more you feel fear, the more you grow. Your fear is the fuel that pushes you to your destination. The more you allow your fears to push you, the stronger you will become. You will learn new skills, interpersonal and intrapersonal. You will learn to survive. It will teach you to differentiate between right and wrong, allowing you to grow yourself into exactly what is required to achieve your goals.

How I Overcame My Fear of Growth

I have lived with many fears. Despite being a workaholic and always loving my work, I always did my best work when I was afraid. I came to realize this and the fact that a lot of my fears of growth revolve around things I have never done before. If I avoid things, my fears grow stronger. But if I attempt them, my fears diminish even when I fail.

For example, I love talking to people, but public speaking always made me uncomfortable. As a child, I was nervous when I had to present something in front of the class. But as I got older, I found myself speaking to groups of people for my job. Now, I speak in front of hundreds of people.

The fear didn't leave me all of a sudden, but I was able to suppress it through practice. I attended public speaking workshops where I was recorded with feedback. I learned valuable tips for being aware of my body language, pronouncing my words correctly, and speaking slowly. These tips have helped me, but what helped me most was constantly pushing myself to engage in public speaking. I could have avoided it if I had tried. But I chose to utilize my fear as fuel.

Many people engage in public speaking every day without any fear at all while I have to actively push myself out of my comfort zone every time. As my audience grew, I began attending public speaking workshops more often, so I could prepare myself against my fear of growth. Of course, I have only described my struggle in a few pages here. In reality, it took me years to understand it all. In my personal life, the fear of growth has overtaken my friendships, relationships, and even going out and meeting new people. I felt very restricted, almost suffocated, in my comfort zone. I knew I had to get out of it to feel alive.

I realized that one of the factors keeping me inside my comfort zone and preventing my growth was the people in my comfort zone. I was too scared to let go of them, but this is what growth demands: to remove parts of yourself that are holding you down. Just like trimming a tree or plant helps it grow better, if we just have the courage to remove parts of ourselves that don't allow our growth, we can thrive in places unknown to us. You will have to remove parts of yourself, especially those that are attached to others, to allow yourself to achieve your goals.

It may sound scary, but let me tell you something we only learn once we go through it: growth brings balance. Yes, it brings more responsibility, even greater uncertainty, but it also brings strength and motivation. You are more likely to succeed when you know that failing isn't even an option. I was never a risk taker. I used to tell others how to succeed in their careers and relationships, but I was afraid of following my own advice. Every time I had an opportunity, I would tell myself that I would pursue it next time. I wasn't ready to be uncomfortable. I would rather stay in my comfort zone than face and deal with my challenges.

But something I realized much later in my journey was that I was facing a lot of challenges. I just didn't think of them as a challenge because they were expected of me. In short, I was facing challenges others posed for me, but I wasn't challenging myself. I was responsible for helping manage several high-end retail stores, each with its own team, yet I managed it smoothly. However, I was too afraid to even set a goal in my personal or professional life. I was just following orders. I handled everything that became my responsibility, but I was always unprepared to be responsible for myself.

I wouldn't change my experience with fear of growth. I took breaks but kept moving forward. I even took some steps back when needed, trying again after some rest. But it was all worth it because it gave me the strength and courage to share my stories and struggles with others. It allowed me to guide others and build the supportive network I always needed.

How to Overcome Fear of Growth

I wrote this book to tell others that it is possible to overcome fears once we take the time to understand them. But we must all take up our own responsibility. I can only guide you and show you that it's not as scary as you might think, but only you can do the work.

That being said, here are some strategies that I believe will prove helpful to you:

Acknowledge Your Fear of Growth

By now you understand that acknowledging any fear is the key to getting over it. I am repeating this strategy only to drive the point home once more. We are often ashamed of our fears, but we don't need to be. Fear is a natural emotion. Apprehension about things unknown is an essential survival response. So, accept that it exists. Just don't accept it in your life to the extent that it stops you.

Make Your Fear Work to Your Advantage

Avoiding the fear of growth never works. Once you have acknowledged it, lean into it and listen to it. It is true that most of our fears are developed through exposure to unnecessary harsh attitudes of those around us, but that's not always the case. Sometimes an unexpected sense of fear can be a gut feeling. It can also be a signal to explore something going on with us that we may be ignoring. So, pay attention to your fear. Listen to what it has to say. See where it's coming from. Does it make sense? Or is it just natural anxiety kicking in? If the case is the latter, pay attention to your anxiety triggers and try to ensure that you are not misunderstanding the cause of your anxiety. Then, let the fear guide you in making better choices.

Let Your Fear Wash Over You

Experience is the best teacher. Experiencing your fear carefully and in a controlled space can help you overcome it much quicker. Here's a story from my life that will allow you to understand how this strategy works:

I wanted to apply for a teaching position at the college of my dreams for many years. I suffered from fear of growth and never had the courage to go through with what I wanted to do. Once I began my journey from fear to fearless, I deliberately allowed my fear of growth to wash over me and stop me from pursuing what I wanted.

I was letting my fears win anyway because I hadn't gotten over them by that time. So, it wasn't like I stepped back on my journey. I merely paused for a while so I could experience the fear in its full capacity. At first, it made me restless and anxious as it always did. Once I gave in to it, I felt a sense of calm. However, the sense of calm faded quicker than I believed it would, and I was left with guilt and regret. I held onto this regret and used it to confront my fear of growth. I told myself over and over that this regret is all I will be left with if I do not get over my fear of growth.

I have to warn you that this strategy can be emotionally draining. However, it works. Sometimes we all need tough love, even from ourselves.

Counter Your Excuses

Our excuses often appear as self-doubt, making us stop in our tracks and wonder if we even deserve what we are pursuing, or if it is something we actually want. Excuses can also take cover behind physical or mental health excuses. They make us believe that we are more tired than we actually are, or that the pending chores will take more time to complete.

Countering excuses only requires some self-awareness. If you feel too tired to, say, work on your book but feel excited to go to the theater to catch the latest blockbuster with your friends the same day, you aren't really tired. Similarly, you can always get up and get the pending chores done while timing yourself. On your desk at home, note down how long each task takes you. You will be surprised at how quickly you get things done once you are in the mental zone to get them out of your way.

However, the best approach is to make time despite all your valid or invalid excuses. Tell yourself that you have to make time for your growth by prioritizing it.

Breathe In Growth

Breathing in growth means surrounding yourself with those who prioritize their growth, i.e., those who have the growth mindset. It sounds clichéd, but it's true that the people a person surrounds themselves with can indicate their priorities. Therefore, if you want to cultivate a growth mindset, seek the company of those who want the same or already have it.

It may be tough to leave your present company and find a new community, but it is essential for your growth as a person. Those who don't want to grow in their lives want others around them to be the same. Consider why parents tell their children to keep good company in school. They know that if their child becomes friends with those who skip classes, he or she will do the same. Similarly, if their child becomes friends with those who care about their grades, participate in contests, and play sports, their child will follow the same path.

Learn From Pain

Life is challenging and painful; there's no doubt about that. The pain we go through can only yield one of two results: it can make us bitter, or it can make us better.

The fact is that nobody likes pain; that's why it makes most of those who experience it bitter. It's understandable, but it isn't right. Pain isn't an experience to enjoy, it is something we need to learn from.

While a lot of people enjoy learning various subjects, it isn't meant to be a relaxing or comfortable experience. Learning through traditional methods such as in classrooms or from tutors isn't easy either. One has to sit for hours, listen to what their teacher has to say, and prove over and over again that they have learned their lesson. Learning is like those unpleasant experiences that yield good outcomes, such as exercising, sitting in saunas, running a marathon, etc.

We may not enjoy the entire spectrum of emotions. We may go to great lengths to avoid pain or negative emotions. But we cannot hide from the fact that life becomes more beautiful, meaningful, and enjoyable when we feel and honor *all* our emotions.

How does that help us grow, you ask? Learning from pain is growth. Our growth as an individual reflects in all aspects of our life and allows us to further improve our life.

Cultivate a Growth Mindset

Growth mindset simply refers to the will to always try things and learn from the results no matter what they turn out to be. Growth never stops. We don't learn from the so-called failures alone. I say so-called because I don't believe in failures. It's not that I don't believe in failure. It's a part of life, but I see these experiences as learning opportunities or stepping stones rather than negative outcomes. I digress, but the point is that we can also learn from our wins.

Understand the Benefits of Growth

Acknowledging the fear enables you to apply the second strategy, which is to understand the benefits of growth. Take your time and reflect on the positive outcomes of personal development. You can also write it all down in a notebook. Analyze how personal development will open doors to bigger and better things. Let the new opportunities excite you.

I believe that anything worth doing is worth doing badly. That's why I don't step back from my fears anymore. Avoiding my goals won't help me since avoidance doesn't get anyone anywhere. It is only through acknowledging our discomfort and attempting it anyway that we can grow.

Fear of Growth as Self-Harm

There's another aspect to fear of growth that isn't discussed enough. It is different from the general understanding and perception of the fear, as people willingly ignore the second aspect. They do this because they don't want to be the person who confesses to experiencing fear of growth in that sense.

Fear of growth in a career or in general keeps us from living our best life, but it doesn't necessarily harm us. I truly believe that a low-key, simple life can be equally as enjoyable and comforting as one spent climbing to the top of the career ladder. In fact, the key to enjoying life is in one's perception and the will to be content and happy. Such an attitude can even make a life full of "apparent" failures a satisfactory one.

But the second aspect of fear of growth is one that harms us, and when we continue to live with it, we make the choice to let ourselves be harmed. This is why nobody wants to confess to having experienced this kind of fear of growth.

The definition of the fear of growth, of course, doesn't change. No matter in what form it is experienced, it is the fear of outgrowing others. But in its second aspect, it means the fear of outgrowing the certainty and the comfortable.

As with any other fear, it develops from thinking too much about what we must not concern ourselves with. When we think of others' points of view when they only bring us harm, we harm ourselves.

Most commonly, the fear of growth expresses itself in this form by keeping us rooted to one place. People born in small towns often grow up wishing to move to metropolitan cities and build a new, different life from the one they have known. However, they rarely do so, because they fear leaving the people and surroundings they are familiar with.

On the other hand, deliberately outgrowing people isn't recommended either. You cannot cut off people simply because you are bored of them or want to experience life in a different way. It is as important to maintain old connections as it is important to form new ones on your journey of personal growth.

You cannot move up in society just through your social circles. You must have the same value to contribute to the room as others in it. As you grow as a person, you also grow as a member of society. Your growth in society will become a positive consequence of your personal growth. However, your resistance to outgrowing people around you who don't want to move ahead in life will also impact your personal growth.

The key is to surround yourselves with those who want to grow in life at the same rate and pace as you. Friends who grow together in their careers and lives are more likely to stick together through the years. Similarly, both people in a relationship must have similar life goals and values to enter a lasting commitment with each other. Besides goals and values, the importance they give to the commitment must also be equal.

6

Fear of Change

———❦———

Change, even good change, can be nerve-wracking. Even when it is a change you have been looking forward to for a while, such as moving to a new city, embarking on a different career path, or starting a new chapter of life, it always comes with uncertainty attached which can make you fear it.

Something that we often don't realize is that change happens constantly, so much so that change is the only constant in our lives. We all change in various ways every day; the world changes in various ways every day too. Everyone goes through it. Everyone experiences it. Some changes are so subtle that we don't always feel them. Let's take the example change in the weather, the most natural phenomenon that everyone on this planet has experienced. It happens constantly. Winter changes into summer and summer into winter by way of spring and fall. Even with extreme weather changes in the last few years due to global warming, the temperature doesn't go from 25 $^{\circ}$F to 95 $^{\circ}$F in one day. The changes in weather are usually gradual.

However, not all changes are subtle. They can be instantaneous and drastic, turning our lives upside down. In fact, it is these changes that make us fear all change in the first place. But here's the thing: nothing is new. It may be new to you, but all humans throughout history have experienced similar changes. In other words, the experiences that make us afraid are those that many before us have experienced already.

For example, we may experience a fear of change when moving to a new city, but this experience is nothing new. Millions have moved from place to place in search of better food, shelter, weather, community, education, and other opportunities throughout the world's history. Hence, it is nothing to be afraid of. It is just a part of life. Sure, it may not be everyone's part of life. But it is a common experience that many people have been through and come out successful and happier.

Moreover, this experience adds new and wonderful things to our lives. It will introduce us to new places and result in meeting new friends. Similarly, starting a new school or job brings a huge change. This change brings new challenges, which push us to prove ourselves and become better during the process.

Why Are People Afraid of Change?

I have observed that people tend to jump to conclusions when thinking about change. Most people imagine change as scary, and though there is a high chance of change being scary, it can also be good. A new job can be scary because we don't want to mess up, but it is still a good change. It can bring us more money and offer more opportunities to make use of our skills. This particular example of change can also bring personal fulfillment and channels to showcase our creativity.

There is no reason to fear change. Change is scary because it is uncertain, but when you think about it, how can something be scary just because it's uncertain? Uncertainty has as many chances of things turning out good as bad. So why are people afraid of it? Why assume the worst and worry when you don't know?

I have to note here that change can feel especially scary when it is imposed on us. For example, throughout human history, people have been forced to leave their homes for political or religious reasons. Of course, nothing can be pleasant when it results from prejudice, hatred, and discrimination. As much as it is important to discuss those changes, they are not the topic of this book. However, I wanted to acknowledge those unpleasant changes because knowledge of them may play a role in how we perceive change.

As mentioned above, the hardest part of change is its uncertainty. There's an equal chance the change will yield either good or bad consequences. Yet even seemingly bad changes can lead to good consequences. Either way, change is inevitable, so we should embrace it and see what it brings. We must learn to notice the subtle changes happening all around us all the time and find comfort in the inevitable progression of life.

How I Overcame My Fear of Change

It took me a long time to understand this concept. I have experienced fear of change for most of my life. I would always assume that change could ruin my life and get scared. I worried about what might happen next. The routine I was in felt comfortable, and I feared that I or others around me wouldn't recognize me if I changed anything. As a result, I lived in the same city for twenty years. But with change as the only constant, I understood that there was no need for me to assume the worst and stay worried.

This habit of fearing change led me to fear many things as an adult woman. For example, I was afraid of wearing my natural hair at work. I always made time to straighten it, even when I didn't want to, when I felt sick or was running late. I was so afraid to look different. When I got older and began wanting to travel the world and see what else was out there, I always stopped myself by asking the what ifs.

It was when I realized how much I was missing out on because of my fears that I began wanting to become a more confident version of myself. Wanting to overcome the fear of change required me to ask myself some tough questions and respond to them honestly. The question I needed to answer most honestly was: *What am I afraid of?* It was affecting me more than I wanted to admit. It began with negative thoughts which turned into negative words. Soon after, those words became feelings of shame and defeat.

This led me to become quiet. I would ignore phone calls, texts, and other methods my friends and family used to reach out to me. Though I could have shared my problems and sought support or help, the changes I was going through felt so overwhelming that I couldn't even bring myself to talk about them. It felt like they would become even stronger and more concrete if I acknowledged them in words.

Of course, the people I cared about cared about me, too, and my behavior worried them. They believed I was avoiding them, or that I didn't want to talk to them or didn't believe they would help me. While none of this was true, it still appeared that way since my beliefs and behavior weren't aligned. I wasn't giving people the same value through my actions as I claimed through my words.

All in all, without even wanting it, I was alienating myself from the people I needed most during my various life transitions. This alienation brought even more changes to my life, changes certain to be unpleasant ones. As a result, the fear of change inside me was putting me through unwanted and unpleasant changes that wouldn't have happened otherwise. I realized I needed to undo this change before it could have any long-term effects on my life. I found it helpful to speak to those near and dear to me. They supported me in more ways than I could imagine, easing the change more than I believed possible.

Many people are afraid of many things. It can be heights, fire, bugs, public speaking, etc. People have common fears and uncommon fears. It doesn't matter. However, what does matter is how much you fear change. Fear of change ranks high on the list of things that trigger anxiety. That's no secret of course. But it is worth exploring why people fear change so much nowadays. Many people will even admit their fear of change openly and more easily than they acknowledge any other fear controlling their life. They will talk about the lengths to which they go to avoid any change taking place in their life. This is surprising, given that so many exciting opportunities await us out there in the twenty-first century. Thus, it is worth exploring why people are so scared of and opposed to change when it is a part of everyday life. Perhaps the problem is not that people fear change but that they fear being changed. Understanding this theory, and the reasons behind it, is essential to overcoming the fear of change. It is what helped me overcome it, and I'm sure it can prove helpful to you, too.

I told myself, "I don't fear change; I fear being changed." This new mantra shaped my perspective about my fear, making it more realistic, even rational. Before understanding this theory, I often stayed silent in rooms where I knew I needed to speak up. I was even afraid to ask for a raise, knowing full well that I had tenured experience and could do any job related to my field amazingly. I was afraid of hearing that I was not a good leader, or I was too young for the position I had achieved or wanted to achieve. Obviously, this fear wasn't helping anyone, least of all me. I was overthinking my ways out of the change I wanted to happen because I was afraid of being changed.

Self-doubt, lack of self-esteem, panic attacks, social anxiety, depression, and the inability to adapt to new situations aside, realizing that change is inevitable is important. I can tell myself that everything at work will remain the same if I don't ask for the promotion I deserve. But who knows? There could be a new manager who has a disagreement with my workstyle; the company could change its structure; economic factors could make surviving on my existing earnings difficult. Anything could happen. Something will happen. My world will change.

The change could be pleasant or unpleasant. It may yield pleasant or unpleasant results. I could only get to know it all if and when something happened. But one thing I could know—and this I memorized—is the fact that things will never remain as they are. Change is inevitable.

How to Let Go of the Fear of Change

Fear of change acts as the root cause of many fears. Hence, it could be difficult to overcome. As you discover your fear of change behind other fears, it might seem bigger to you and even impossible to overcome. I won't tell you it's not challenging, but I will tell you that it is definitely possible. In fact, there are three techniques for letting go of fear of change that I want to share with you.

Now, before you say to yourself, *"I don't need to read this; I don't suffer from fear of change,"* think again. You may not want to or like to, but at some level, you suffer from fear. How can I say this? Because everyone suffers from fear. Fear of change is the most common fear because nobody knows the future. Fear of change is the fear of the unknown. It doesn't matter if all your previous plans have worked out. It doesn't matter how thorough you are with planning. The results of something you put effort into are always uncertain. Hence, even if the chances are minute, there's always a chance things might not go your way.

The young may seem unafraid compared to those in their 30s, 40s, or even older. Yet there are more uncertainties in their lives than their older peers. What will you do after high school? Will you go to college? What college will you attend? How much money will you earn in your job? Where are you going to live? What car will you drive? If you are a young person and have it all planned out already, tell me: *how will you adjust to anything that doesn't go according to your plan?*

On the other hand, if you have spent considerable years as an adult, tell me: *are you still trying to achieve the things you planned when you were in high school?*

These questions are tough. Life will happen to you because it happens to everybody. You might start making excuses for how everything changed instead of admitting how your own actions played a part. You may not want to take any action in overcoming the issues that led to the failure of your plans. You may indulge in self-doubt, wondering if you ever deserved anything you ever wanted or if you even had it in yourself to make it happen.

That's where I want you to stop. Stop thinking negative things. Do the following three things:

1. Let go of self-doubt.

Self-doubt causes a lack of confidence in one's abilities or judgement. It takes place when we compare ourselves to others and set unrealistic expectations for ourselves that don't align with multiple factors in our lives.

Life happens to everyone, but we can always take action to change it. Change will take place anyway. Don't restrict your life to the bad ones. Did some unpleasant change take place in your life? Grieve over it, then get over it. Take some actions to bring about a good change in your life. The best results come from making changes. Try it.

2. Change your mindset.

Fear is often a result of negative thinking patterns, such as catastrophizing, black and white thinking, and mindreading (or trying to mindread). These patterns tend to lead to a self-fulfilling prediction: they make you believe in the worst-case scenario, and you act accordingly.

Changing the mindset, i.e., breaking away from the negative thinking pattern, is the key to not allowing your fears to ruin your life. To change your mindset, you need to challenge your negative thoughts and replace them with positive ones. For example, if you have a fear of failure, you could challenge the thought, "I will never succeed" by asking yourself, "What evidence do I have to support this thought?" Here's a fact: there is zero evidence that can predict your failure certainly. Even if you have failed in the same test previously, many factors must have changed between your past and present. In fact, challenging yourself may even make you realize that you have succeeded in the past in various other tests. You may also acknowledge that failure is a natural part of the learning process. This will help you feel optimistic, hopeful, and confident.

Moreover, it can help you develop a growth mindset. A growth mindset allows you to see every failure as an opportunity to learn and grow. All your failures are experiences. You may not pass the test, but you can learn how to fail it. It isn't entirely useless to know how to fail a test. Remember it and don't repeat it.

Growth mindset enables you to see the silver lining even on the darkest of days. It encourages you to go after your goals with a refreshed motivation and get over all your fears, including the fear of change. This brings you confidence, resilience, and higher self-esteem. Once you achieve the persistence that growth mindset offers, you will be filled with determination and get over any (new) fear you might acquire.

3. Don't put all your eggs in one basket.

For the areas of life where you can exercise control, don't hesitate to do so. In my observation, we often try to control things we cannot while giving up what control we do possess. It makes me wonder whether we really want to control things in the first place, or if it is just the idea of control that we like.

I digress, but the point remains the same: move forward with caution where you can. This can especially feel helpful for professional changes. For example, it is not wise to quit your present job to pursue your dream job. If you do, you risk being unemployed. You can start from scratch in your dream career, but don't sit idle. In fact, do more than one thing. Spend your energy on more than one venture until your dream career comes to life. Some might call it *playing it safe*, but playing safe is better than feeling overwhelmed. Don't care about what others say about your methods to conquer your fear. This is your journey. Nobody else is going to walk it for you. Since you are the only person who can get your life together, do whatever you can to make the process easier.

You don't owe any explanations to anyone. You don't have to make your journey more difficult than it is to gain anyone's recognition or praise. Stop caring what others think and do what's best for you.

Diversify your life. Take this from someone who has spent most of her life living with various fears. There is always more out there; more options, ventures, methods, and paths. Since you are reading this book, I think it's safe to assume you are an overthinker like me. This is why I tell you not to put your mind at risk for one venture when there are many. Until you gain the confidence to face drastic changes by giving your all, it is best to keep space to move backwards and take other paths when needed.

I will say it again: don't hesitate to apply this method thinking of what people might say about you. Those who truly care about you will give you the same advice I am giving you here. Who will rescue you if you burn all the bridges and get stuck in the fire? Nobody. So don't burn the bridges. Explore your options like a tourist in a new city. Window shop everywhere before you select an outlet to make your purchase. You are the one who is paying for your life decisions with your energy and time. Don't listen to those who you haven't asked for advice.

All in all, the challenge with change comes from our tendency to see it as a problem rather than an opportunity to learn and grow. However, it is also worth remembering that change isn't supposed to be easy since life isn't supposed to be easy. But with change comes elevation; it is only by remembering this fact that we can grow out of our fear of change.

The truth is that we cannot live without change. Change is inevitable, the only constant. We cannot avoid it or prevent it from happening. So, getting over the fear of change is the only solution. Overcoming this fear is a process. It takes time. Some days, you will feel the fear is strengthened and overwhelming while on other days, you will feel as if you never suffered from it. Be open to living both kinds of days. Allow yourself to go through the process to make it to the other side.

Embrace your journey. Become flexible to accommodate change as it happens. Own what life throws at you. In time, you will learn to see it as a natural part of life. Keep living your life. No change will stop it, but every change will teach you a lot about your life. Learn and make use of the knowledge you acquire. Use it as fuel for success. Not everything will go as you plan, but your success is inevitable as you learn to embrace change and make the best of every situation. You will figure out how to look for opportunities in everything that happens to you. Own what change brings for you and wait for the next change to get more from life.

I urge you to challenge your mindset. Let change shake you. Allow yourself to see what it has to offer. There is so much out there on the other side of fear.

7

Fear of Focus

Fear of focus is, on a pragmatic level, quite real. It's instilled in us by the thought that our focus isn't nearly enough. We may worry that our focus will not produce results and that we will leave people wanting more. Perhaps ironically, fear of focus may turn out to be the cause of our failure to produce acceptable results.

Specialization or inherent focus on just one thing can mean a buildup of knowledge pertaining to a particular subject or topic. This also means we may limit ourselves to the depth of information available.

While people may not fear the art of focusing on a linear pattern, they can feel an association hindering their ability to focus or produce results. The process of focusing entails many aspects within itself that can contribute to feeling skeptical when it comes to placing our focus on one specific. Such specifics can include the following:

What if we're not good at it?

Feeling as if our focus may not reap rewards can contribute to a debilitating emotional wavelength. We may find ourselves in a pickle with no way out if the one particular we focus on does not reward us the way we require it to. Focusing on just one thing can also limit our credibility.

We sometimes want to be part of a variety of possibilities. If we don't succeed at focusing on one thing, we may believe the problem lies in us, and we cannot focus on anything. The issue at hand here is not the idea of focusing but feelings of unworthiness that feed our fear.

Can we focus?

We may have a natural tendency to steer off topic. If we limit our life and routine to focusing on one particular aspect of our daily unwind, we may steer off topic completely and lose focus. Losing focus ultimately entails being unable to finish our current task. However, since that's all we've committed to, we can find ourselves struggling to come to terms with ourselves. It's the mere thought of feeling unfocused and forecasting what our future may look like.

Feeling overwhelmed.

There's a chance we may feel overwhelmed by the mere concept of focus. We may place undue pressure on ourselves to attain success on a specific factor. Placing all our attention on maintaining focus can lead us astray because we don't focus on completing the task at hand but rather fear our ability to complete it.

Fear breeds feelings of inadequacy. When we have a fear of focus, we believe we don't have the capacity to follow through with a task. This can restrict us from performing a task even before we curate a plan to move forward.

Fear of Focus Compared to Other Fears

It is useful to compare fear of focus to other fears since they can sometimes get confused. Suffice it to say that fear of focus comes close to some other fears, and may even be included in others, but it stands as its own syndrome. Let's take a look at how fear of focus can be distinguished.

Perfectionism

Since fear of focus is often considered obsessive, it lines us up with the fear of perfectionism. There is, in fact, a slim line between fear of focus and fear of perfectionism. Perfectionists tend to be highly critical, setting a standard that may be impossible to achieve. In that way, perfectionism can be like the fear of focus. Yet perfectionists do tend to pursue the project; they just never achieve satisfaction. Those with fear of focus become so obsessed with "being good enough" that it causes them not to even get started. One forms a characteristic quality entailing fear while the other breeds fear without any evidence.

Fear of Commitment

Fear of focus can be somewhat related to fear of commitment, but there's one major difference: the fear of focus does not have to involve being afraid of commitment. The fear of commitment label is usually applied to shying away from closeness in intimate relationships, but it's more than that. Fear of commitment can apply to any venture requiring promise of ongoing or regular presence. Like other fears, fear of commitment can be related to abandonment.

Fear of focus should not be confused with fear of commitment. Commitment is a healthy approach in life; obsessiveness is not. Since fearing focus involves obsessiveness, it can breed as part of the fear of commitment; however, it does not fall within the same spectrum. By the same token, fear of commitment cannot be flagged under fear of focus because the two have no direct association.

Fear of Success

Fear of success can also be loosely termed fear of achievement. In simple terms, we can fear success before experiencing it because we tend to analyze how our new life would ultimately change our status quo. How will success change my relationships? Will I lose the people I love? Will it be tougher for me to establish healthier relationships? Will I ever find a way to reach out to my genuine connections, or will they move past me? Will their intentions with me change? Having a fear of success is legitimate because it has a strong correlation to the fear of change. However, it is not associated with the fear of focus because that falls within the obsessiveness corridor. Meanwhile, fear of success is simply a dread associated with change and the unfamiliarity and discomfort it brings.

Fear of success comes in the shape of a few qualities mentioned below:

1. Not having goals

When an individual sets no real goals for themselves, they actually set the bar so low that success has no way of leveling up to them. It's also seen as a defense mechanism to restrict any growth from entering the spectrum.

2. Giving up almost instantaneously

People who give up easily don't do it out of fear of losing but as a coping mechanism to avoid change and practically any form of growth. It's easier to not make any appreciable headway that would reap results. If success rears its scary head, they just quit. Quitting may seem a lot like losing, but it's a sigh of relief for those who fear achievement and all that it brings with it.

3. Procrastination

Delaying a certain action or process has a lot to do with an attempt to refrain from doing something. This is the opposite of obsessively focusing on something. The focus here may be headstrong, but it hasn't as much to do with obsessively eyeing one key feature as not following through with one's work. As part of a defense mechanism, procrastination is heavily based on self-sabotage which is a way of avoiding success.

Certain key characteristics may indicate a fear of success. It may involve worry over something getting more complicated than what one can presumably handle. It may also involve overthinking how to approach the project to the point it never gets started. The thing to keep in mind is that, like other fears, fear of success can hide behind other concerns we create or exaggerate in our minds.

Fear of Focus and Change of Space

According to research, a change in space can lead to release of information we are holding, replacing it with new information. The theory makes complete sense as a change in space leads to a change of stimuli. When we enter a new space, we subconsciously pick up a lot of new information. Of course, a new space doesn't mean a strange space. It simply means a change of space from one to another, even if we can navigate the *new* space with our eyes closed. Hence, when we walk from our bedroom to the kitchen for a specific purpose, we tend to forget why we entered the kitchen in the first place. We stand there lost and confused, and even a little mad at ourselves. But we shouldn't be. We have evolved to survive, and the act of our brain shedding old information to make room for new is only one of the ways through which our species has survived.

Before we talk about this fear of focus further, I want you to know that there's no shame in choosing an easier path to ensure your survival. Life happens to us all the time, even when we aren't ready to face it. The beauty of life lies in always having the opportunity to correct our course and do what we should have done in the first place. With that, let's take a look at fear of focus developed from worry and stress.

Development of Fear of Focus from Constant Stress

Our soft focus can be severely negatively impacted by constant worry and stress. It happens as the part of our brain responsible for soft focus gets bombarded with more information than it can make sense of. Sensory overload lasting for a long time can leave the brain tired and overwhelmed. This develops in us a fear of focus since we are designed and evolved to conserve energy to ensure our survival, meaning that our brains and bodies reject activities that can leave us feeling vulnerable.

Research has shown that the ability to focus is negatively impacted in direct proportion to the amount of stress we are experiencing. An example of this correlation is the way we forget details of an unfortunate accident.

For example, immediately after an accident, a person may clearly remember specific details like the weather conditions, or the exact time or the color of the other vehicle involved. However, as weeks or months pass these specific details often become fuzzy or are completely forgotten, even though the emotional impact or the overall event remains in memory.

The fact we cannot recall details of what happened even before we experienced the accident is further proof of the correlation between fear and the inability to focus. It happens because of sensory overload caused by our brain trying to stay calm, understand the situation, and figure out multiple survival techniques all at the same time.

This isn't meant to make you feel bad about your mind. The human brain is extraordinarily powerful and can accomplish a lot more than these tasks in any given moment. Fear is what cripples our mind in such circumstances. But you can unlearn the pattern that has led to your inability to focus and relearn how to maintain focus. You must only be ready to do it.

That being said, it is essential to acknowledge that stress and worry are experiences that everyone goes through. Like other bodily and mental functions, these are survival tools. They allow us to sense potential harm and danger and do something about them. They help us navigate situations that require us to be swift. Therefore, you must not try to expect yourself to never feel stressed again. Instead, the goal is to understand how your mind works and take charge of it to live your best life.

Understanding the Bias of the Human Brain

Fear of focus can be overcome, as can other fears discussed in this book. It only requires accepting some cold facts and understanding certain realities of life. Once you do that, you will overcome all fears including the fear of focus. Moreover, you will learn to utilize fear as the survival tool it is meant to be.

The first fact I want you to accept is your own brain's bias. We all want to be trusting and optimistic, but we couldn't have survived as a species if that's how we were. We survived because of our negative thoughts. Our doubts, selfishness, and pessimism contributed a lot to us surviving and thriving. Therefore, embracing these negative thoughts and feelings is the first step toward overcoming fear.

We often mistake "embrace" for granting the permission to take control, but that's a misconception. Embracing our feelings simply means accepting them as they are without wanting to suppress them. When we embrace our fears, we don't have to let them take charge of our actions and lives. Instead, we can acknowledge their presence as a survival tool. Our fears are our instincts looking out for us. We can be thankful for their existence and move on.

As individuals trying to make the best of our lives, we must accept our emotions to utilize them to our advantage. I'm sure that, like me, you have ignored or suppressed your emotions from time to time. We all know how that goes: the emotions confront us by becoming stronger and more intense, so much so that we lose control of them. This happens because we are hardwired to ensure our own survival.

On the other hand, when we acknowledge our emotions, we prevent them from getting stronger to the extent that they can take control over us. We send a signal to our mind that we have noted its effort to ensure our safety and that we appreciate this effort. By paying attention to our negative emotions, we help slow their bombardment of our brain, thus providing our mind the time and conditions it needs to make rational decisions.

We can use the time we have after acknowledging our emotions to inform ourselves more about the situation. For example, deep sea diving and snorkeling are adventurous sports that can be rewarding. However, we may feel scared the first time we want to experience them. The fear can be overwhelming, making us back out. If we ignore or suppress the fear, we put ourselves at risk of making a mistake during the adventure. In this circumstance, the best strategy is to acknowledge the fear and inform our mind that we are making a conscious choice and aren't faced with danger as it may perceive it. The intentionality of the situation can prepare our minds so that instead of being scared we become vigilant which, in turn, will increase our focus.

How to Overcome Fear of Focus

We cannot function or live for long without any of the amazing processes our minds and bodies have evolved to perform. We may not find every function or emotion we experience pleasant, but that doesn't make any of them less important than others.

The key to overcoming any fear—especially the fear of focus—is to understand your own mind. When you get to the root of everything you experience, whether physically, mentally, or emotionally, you will find yourself able to control your mind as you wish.

Your consciousness is the command center for your existence. Your brain and nervous system houses the various mechanisms that bring consciousness into existence and make it worth enjoying. While consciousness originates from interdependence of the mind and body, it is something bigger and higher than both combined.

Instill this perspective within yourself to create the life you are meant to have. That's right: life happens to you, but you also make your life happen. You are a lot more in control than you believe. Trust your authority. There's nothing that can get in your way once you want it. You only need to believe that you can do it.

Our realities are shaped by our perspectives. A shift in mindset is all we need to make our life the way we want it to be. However, we cannot be successful by choosing some functions over others. We must accept all that our mind and body offer—good, bad, or ugly—and learn to use everything to our advantage. Once we acknowledge that stress is normal, our competitive spirit will take over to redirect our focus to the problem at hand. After that, the rest of the process becomes easy.

Can't focus? Find activities that snatch your focus!

Though technology has its uses, here I must talk about its drawbacks, and more specifically, social media. Created as a tool of communication and connection, social media has become a hobby for the majority of people with access to it. This is an unfortunate fact about the modern world. We have forgotten our actual hobbies and the joy they used to bring us. I know this well because I was one of the people who would spend all their free time scrolling through one social media app or another. It was only when I wanted to get over my fears that I noticed how much harm social media was doing to me and my focus.

Not that social media is a bad thing per se; it's just that we are bombarded with information every moment we use it. To regain our focus, we must take back the time we spend on social media. We can't allow our minds to get overwhelmed and ultimately exhausted by information it doesn't need. Instead, let's reclaim our time and attention. Just like we can accept our negative emotions and thoughts and use them to our advantage, we can also use technology to our advantage. Everything has its pros and cons; it's up to us to decide what we want to get from it.

So, put down your smartphone and pick up activities that don't overwhelm you. Read more, take up gardening, practice yoga, or just exercise. Once you feel less afraid of focusing on one thing at a time, you might pick up your old hobbies. What did you enjoy doing before you got your first smartphone? If you are a young person who was handed a smartphone at an early age, you might try new hobbies until you find something interesting. Make art, dance, run, build something from scratch, recycle, watch sports, or learn a musical instrument. There's so much more to life beyond a screen.

Once you find some hobbies, you will realize that focusing on something was never really that difficult. Your mind just needed to get past all the attention-grabbing stimuli. After it does, you'll find that your mind is no longer afraid to focus. Now you should allow yourself the pleasure of being lost in something you truly enjoy. Read until you lose track of time, focus on your art until you forget to eat, be so involved in your passion that it becomes your existence. Such focus is absolutely possible. You will be able to achieve it, and more, if you simply allow your body and mind to function as they are supposed to and take up your authority over them.

But there's one more thing you must do before you try to overcome your fear of focus: make sure you aren't suffering from any other fear. There's a reason I'm discussing the fear of focus last in this book. You may perceive any of your other fears as fear of focus; however, it isn't difficult to differentiate. All you need to do is deal with your fears one at a time.

The journey may be slow, but steadiness will ensure your success. Don't be in a rush, even if you feel that your fears have made you miss your life. Avoid overwhelming yourself, whether intentionally or unintentionally. Learn the art of slow living and prioritize progress over winning.

The journey from fear to fearless is beautiful, walk it consciously and unafraid to enjoy everything it has to offer.

The concept of fear is dug in thousands of feet under us. Over millennia, it branched out and found a way to participate in practically every concept of our life. By its basic and untainted definition, the feeling of fear is essentially our emotional reaction to something that may pose a danger to ourselves. Feeling threatened within ourselves, and due to our own key characteristics, is a debilitating thought to live with.

Our brains and bodies are meant to protect us; the signals within them work almost instantaneously. Indeed, our actions are motivated by a need to protect against outside danger, a need that was instilled in us thousands of years ago. Nonetheless, we can train our minds not to feel threatened by even the slightest change. How we train our mind and soul to view matters differently is how we ultimately get a hold on the actions we take. Once we've sorted that out, whether it's the fear of focus, perfectionism, achievement, success, or the relationship all of them share with each other, we find ourselves standing on much calmer ground. Falling down to our knees in the face of our fear may free us for a few hours, but the compulsiveness will come back stronger, and that's essentially what we have to reduce.

We cannot submit to our pain or what we're afraid of. More important, we cannot avoid change because doing so will inevitably push us into a deeper, darker hole. Consider it like training for your brain. You've got to train your brain to face the music, face the pain, and face fear headlong and at eye level. That's when we break the chain.

If we do not rise up to the challenge, it doesn't matter how much success we find for ourselves. What matters at the end of the day is how we find the ability to own our growth. Knowing our worth and rejecting unhealthy defense mechanisms is the real win here. Once you target that with a willingness and intent to win, your fears will automatically lose all their power.

You'll be surprised to see your growth and how you now didn't bend in tough times but instead rose to the occasion. That's where growth happens, when we go in for a fight knowing it may go either way, but we're not afraid of the result. Growth also happens when we have enough confidence in our ability not only as human beings but as individuals who have festered and regrown their strength from scratch by nurturing their inner child and future self.

I wrote this book to share my journey of overcoming my fears with the intent of helping people. I really hope you, my reader, have learned something from my journey from fear to fearless.

I will leave with a quote I read a long time ago that summarizes my message:

"He who fears to suffer, suffers from fear."

Don't let yourself suffer. Get the upper hand on fear. Rule it and it won't rule you!

Best wishes.

YOU CAN HAVE IT ALL; JUST NOT ALL AT ONCE!